British Big Cats- The Early Years
by Jan Williams

• *Mystery cat researcher for longer than she cares to remember, and still looking for an answer which fits all the facts. Married, 2 children. Hates publicity.*

1976 is a date set in stone in mystery cat research – the year in which the Dangerous Wild Animals Act was introduced and, according to popular theory, the year in which British big cats originated. It certainly had an impact on the situation, as there was a major increase in the number of reports and the areas affected around that time.

It's difficult to judge now just how much of this increase was due to newly-released animals, and how much to increased publicity encouraging people to come forward with sightings of cats which were already there. Big cats were being seen well before 1976, though the records are few and far between in comparison to today.

One aspect that hasn't changed, however, is the confusion as to exactly what was being seen. The cat seen by young William Cobbett in the eighteenth century, which he later compared to a Canadian lynx, could have been a surviving English wildcat; there are suggestions that the species hung on till a late date in the thick woodlands of Surrey and Sussex. The sketch which accompanied the newspaper report of the supposed lynx killed in Inverness in 1927 looks more like a caracal, commonly known as the African lynx, and the description - "yellow(...)without spots upon its coat" - sounds more like this species than the European lynx with which it has been identified.

This confusion has continued into more recent times. The variation in markings displayed by some of the smaller cat species makes definite identification very difficult. The cat shot near Widecombe in 1988 still had some milk teeth. Leopard cats normally lose their milk teeth by the age of six months, yet this animal was the size of an adult leopard cat. The body of the cat shot at Kingsley in 1981 was taken to the University of Liverpool veterinary field station where it was identified as an ocelot by Helen King, wife of Professor J.O.L. King, Vice President of the North of England Zoological Society, and an acknowledged expert on exotic cats in her own right; yet has now been recorded as another leopard cat. Only a few years ago it was impossible to differentiate between small cat species using DNA testing, and hair analysis still has its limitations. Both depend on someone first recognising a specimen as unusual, and then getting the testing done.

THE OTHER BLACK PANTHER

Understanding exactly which cat species are living wild in Britain is becoming increasingly important as reported sightings increase. An overwhelming number of reports now relate to 'black panthers'. Some of these black cats look like black leopards, and others have the features of a small cat (Felis) species, though exactly which one is a matter of continuing debate.

I first saw a black panther in Cheshire in 1973. I didn't know much about exotic cats at the time and assumed it was a black leopard. It may indeed have been one, possibly the one that Leslie Maiden claimed to have released at Snake Pass in Derbyshire that same year. It was more than twenty years before I was lucky enough to see one again, and in the intervening years I studied exotic cats of all kinds, visiting many zoos in this country and abroad to see as many different species as possible. So that, on the day when a 'log' in the next field finally stood up, stretched, and revealed itself as a dog-sized black panther, I was able to say with certainty that this one was not a leopard.

On a sunny Autumn afternoon a few years later, a third black panther walked out onto a path directly in front of my son and I. It seemed as surprised and interested to see us as we undoubtedly were to see it, and paused for a few seconds with its body sideways on and its head turned towards us. It was slightly longer and taller than a Labrador dog, with jet-black glossy fur and a slender torso. The head was shaped like a small cat species, the ears were pointed and without tufts, and the tail, held downwards with a slight upward curl at the end, would have been just about long enough to reach the ground.

This cat was not any of the usual suspects, not leopard or jaguar, lynx or Asian jungle cat. Nor was it an oversized domestic – though if I'd had a camera I'm fairly sure the reaction to any photo would have been that it was an unusual domestic cat. Short of persuading one to stand right next to a yardstick, I'm not sure how it's possible to get past that problem. I couldn't match it to any cat species I've ever seen, though golden cats would probably come closest and I'd like to see a melanistic caracal to know whether the gene also affects the ear and tail length. It did, however, correspond to reports made by other witnesses over the years.

BIG CATS
IN BRITAIN
YEARBOOK
2006
edited by Mark Fraser

Edited by Susan Marsh and Jonathan Downes
Cover and internal design by Mark North for CFZ Communications
Using Microsoft Word 2000, Microsoft , Publisher 2000, Adobe Photoshop CS.

First published in Great Britain by CFZ Press

CFZ Press
Myrtle Cottage
Woolfardisworthy
Bideford
North Devon
EX39 5QR

CFZ PRESS

© CFZ MMVI

ISBN: 978-1-905723-01-0

CONTENTS

Foreword *by Nigel Brierly*   5

British Big Cats The Early Years *by Jan Williams*   7

The South Devon Polygon *by Chris Moiser*   13

Argyll Big Cats 2005 *by Shaun Stevens*   23

Gloucestershire Big Cats *by Trystan Swale*   27

Cats, Tracks and Trials *by Alan White*   33

Northumbrian Big Cat Diaries *by Ian Bond*   41

DNA *by Chris Johnston*   43

Faeces from a Leopard *by Mark Fraser*   47

Mystery Cat Diary 2005 compiled *by Mark Fraser*

      January   59

      Februry   71

      March   79

      April   89

      May   103

      June   115

      July   127

      August   135

      September   145

      October   157

      November   169

      December   175

Foreword
by Nigel Brierly

In 1983, a major incident occurred on several farms situated on the southern edge of Exmoor. Multiple sheep killings took place - the work of unknown predators - and the marines were called in to hunt the culprits down. The story hit the headlines in both the national and local press: the 'Beast of Exmoor" was born.

Over the next twenty years or so, the public gradually realised that big cats were roaming throughout Britain. The press dubbed them as 'beasts' wherever they were sighted. The number of big cat researchers also rose from a handful to the hundreds we have today. Big cat researching has become almost an addiction, and those actively involved have found it to be both exciting and enjoyable.

Mark Fraser formed the Big Cats in Britain Research Group just at the time it was needed. The Group aimed to bring big cat researchers together to exchange their experiences in the field and share their expertise, a process essential to gaining a clearer picture of what is happening to the wild cats in Britain, and indeed, how many species are out there. Both are complex questions and pose a real challenge.

My hope is that the BCIB group will progress and that members will succeed in coming up with at least some of the answers.

Nigel Brierly
November 2005

Lumping different species of cat together can create both confusion and potential problems. Wild-living pumas have been clearly described by some well-qualified witnesses, and prints and signs have been found. Besides the well known kills and capture of lynx, one was found dead in a fox snare in the Orbliston Forest in Moray in 1975. Jim A Johnston suggested (The Skerray Beast, Scots Magazine, 1979) that it was the result of a covert attempt to reintroduce lynx to the Highlands. There were reports of lynx-like cats in London suburbs years before Lara was captured, and it's interesting to note that the finding of decapitated foxes (known lynx behaviour) in the wild and overgrown Highgate cemetery was one of the triggers which sparked the Highgate Vampire case in the late 1960s.

Similarly there is good evidence that some of the black panthers sighted are indeed leopards. Believing that all of them are, however, is bound to create exactly the kind of confusion that is being seen today. Sightings, but a lack of leopard-sized prints; purported attacks with only minor injuries; kills with only a small amount of meat taken; photos dismissed as domestic cats, and a lot of unhappy witnesses ridiculed for describing what they saw.

It may also create both unnecessary panic, as the press trumpet stories of hundreds of leopards rampaging across the countryside; and, perhaps, an unfounded sense of security in assuming that large numbers of leopards have lived here for many years and never caused any serious problems, and therefore will not do so in the future. The great majority of wild leopards, as we know, are elusive animals, which do their best to avoid contact with people, but all of them are potentially powerful predators. As the situation stands, one serious attack is likely to cause a kneejerk reaction throughout the country.

UNNATURAL HISTORY

Establishing exactly what the second black panther is has proved remarkably difficult, with proposals ranging from giant feral domestic cats, an unknown black variant of the puma or some other species, hybrids, or a completely unknown species, to, more simply, witnesses exaggerating the size of domestics or misreporting the features of the animals.

Hybridisation between cat species, especially in the wild, has been a touchy subject with zoologists for many years, although the recent discovery through DNA testing of wild-born hybrids between bobcats and Canadian lynx, has opened up discussion. There is good evidence for puma/leopard hybrids born in captivity, and one known case of three litters of puma/ocelot cubs born in South America. Serval/caracal hybrids are also known, and a number of small cats have successfully hybridised with domestic cats. Geoffroy's cat/domestic hybrids are particularly interesting, in that the offspring (known as Safari cats) grow much larger than either parent, reaching weights of 25- 30lbs.

In terms of a single species, one issue is the overwhelming number of black animals, as well as some of the more peculiar colour patterns reported. Unusual colour varieties tend to occur when animals are isolated geographically, as with the black rabbits and blonde hedgehogs of Alderney, in the Channel Islands. However, it takes time for these changes to occur.

Between the Ice Age origin proposed by Di Francis, and the DWA of 1976, there is a range of other ways in which an exotic species could have been introduced to the British Isles. Early menageries and travelling circuses are one possibility often mentioned, and sailors brought animals back with them from foreign climes to sell at ports like Liverpool and London. Exotic species of all kinds, many rare today, were freely available to the public in Victorian times. And in the colonial era, men returning from overseas postings brought back a variety of pets, including leopards, ocelots and golden cats, some of which were donated to zoos.

The fashion for fur coats in the 1950s and 60s decimated wild cat populations around the world. In 1968 alone, for example, American fur traders imported 129,000 ocelot pelts. Cat species which are very rare now would have been much more common in the early years of this century. Our attitude towards animals has changed enormously even in the last few years, as we have come to accept the need for conservation and seen the damage that can be done by introducing alien animals to fragile environments. Earlier generations had a much more casual attitude to such things.

Alien species have been breeding in the UK for centuries. We live amongst them. Rabbits, grey squirrels, little owls, muntjac deer, and, of course, our domestic cats, breed and thrive here more successfully than some of our native species. A small cat species could have been introduced in sufficient numbers to create a breeding group by one of the above means, and, given an initial small gene pool and enough time, produced a widespread population of mystery panthers. But introduction is only part of the problem – most of our alien species were welcomed and encouraged, at least initially, and their presence is very obvious. Staying hidden presents a much more difficult challenge.

GIANT FERAL CATS

When the Surrey Puma first leapt into the public imagination, a strange belief was current in natural history circles. Experienced naturalists confidently stated that domestic cats which took to living wild sometimes grew to huge sizes. Unlike record-breaking domestic cats which tend to be heavily overweight, these feral beasts were much larger in size, massively muscled, and dined on rabbits and lambs instead of smaller prey.

In 1977, renowned naturalist Sir Christopher Lever reiterated this belief: "In the wild the descendants of domestic cats often increase considerably in size and frequently become as fierce as the true wild cat." (*The Naturalised Animals of the British Isles*, Hutchinson, London, 1977). Dr Maurice Burton mentions the belief that large sizes and intense ferocity are produced by the second generation of 'gone wild' cats. (*Wild Animals of the British Isles*; Frederick Warne, London, 1968)

Studies carried out over the past thirty years have failed to find any evidence for these ideas. For instance, Roger Tabor's study of cats in England showed that feral cats have a similar weight range to normal domestic cats, and he concluded that in terms of both weight and length, the English feral cat is hardly different from the average domestic cat. (*The Wildlife of the Domestic Cat*; Arrow, London, 1983). As a result, the belief in giant feral cats has quietly disappeared from mainstream theory, and been consigned to the realm of folklore.

But folklore, whilst distorted and confused, often has a basis in fact. How and why did these stories arise? Could they provide the missing link to help make sense of today's reports?

Dr Maurice Burton's comments on the subject sound surprisingly familiar. He says that gamekeepers are the best source of information on the subject of huge feral cats, but that they know how to keep a still tongue, and even when they do talk you find their main interest has been to bury the carcass as soon as possible. They don't take measurements, so for size you have to be content with 'enormous', 'big as a dog' and 'twice as big as an ordinary cat'. The only one he was able to study at close quarters himself 'in a remote wood in Devon' seemed enormous, and its size was matched by its ferocity.

He recounts a friend's experience of seeing a 'large black fox' throw a rabbit in the air. Through binoculars it proved to be a huge black cat. The man's assessment of its size was that it made his own tomcat look like a kitten, and his cat weighed 21 lbs. Dr Burton's skepticism regarding the Surrey Puma reports, and his belief they could be explained by feral cats begins to seem more understandable.

The publicity caused by a big cat sighting can often produce reports of other, less spectacular, animals. Many of these sightings can be dismissed as normal wildlife, but some raise further questions. During a big cat flap on the Isle of Wight in the 1980s, Mrs. Whitehead of Freshwater wrote to the *County Press* regarding the huge cats seen on Yarmouth Marsh in the 1940s. She told me that, as a child, she lived in a house backing onto the marsh and that the cats were seen there over a period of about three years. She only saw one once herself and thought at first that it was a dog because of its size, but then realised it was an outsized cat, twice the size of a big tomcat. Her father and uncle used to see them stalking along the fence of the chicken run at night, and were so concerned by their size and ferocity that they wouldn't let her go out into the garden in case one came. Other people in the area caught a glimpse of them from time to time, and their calls were heard; an unearthly wailing noise, "like a high-pitched wowee". Three of their domestic cats went missing at this time, and one ginger cat returned "torn to shreds" and had to be put down.

Another huge cat that killed domestic cats and lambs was shot at Great Witley in Worcestershire in 1962. Describing it years later, the man (who had been fourteen at the time) was quite certain it was an English Wildcat, and refused to believe that they had been extinct for many years. It was, he said, twice as big as a large tomcat, with a short blunt-ended tail and long fangs that stuck out at the sides of its mouth. He'd never seen anything like it before or since, despite acting as an unofficial vermin killer for most of the local farmers.

PUMA TIME BEGINS

The publicity surrounding the Surrey Puma saga triggered reports from nearby counties; a labrador-sized cat with pointed ears, seen crossing a road at Preston Candover, near Alton, Hampshire in 1959; black panther-like cats reported by gamekeepers at Farley Mount and Kings Somborne, to the west of Winchester; and big cats at Nettlebed, Oxfordshire, and Stoke Poges and Littleworth Common in Buckinghamshire, all in 1964.

In the area around Ewshot, the centre of the Surrey puma sightings, at least four different cats were reported, only one of which matched the description of a puma. Of the others, one was a smaller sandy-coloured animal, dismissed as a feral cat by Dr Maurice Burton and possibly the animal photographed at Worplesdon; a second spotted and striped cat was described as similar to a small cheetah or long-tailed lynx, and the third was a very large black cat.

It didn't matter – from this point on they were all lumped together as 'pumas'. Had some of them previously been hiding under the banner of 'giant feral cats'?

The South Devon Polygon
by Chris Moiser

● *Chris is a professional zoologist and the author of four books, including three on our British mystery cats. He was born in Berkshire and has been researching the mystery big cat phenomena since the early 1990s. He was recently responsible for exposing a national hoax and works hard at trying to discover just what is out there!*

Being based in Plymouth it seemed only natural that I should study the alien big cat phenomena in my immediate area. There was the Beast of Bodmin to the West, and the Beast of Exmoor to the North, but the lesser known sightings were right on my doorstep, to the East of the City of Plymouth.

When I initially started studying these animals I was teaching full time at the local College of Further Education. This was quite useful, because it gave me access to a modest number of people who had expertise in other areas, and to a vast number of students, some of whom were more than happy to be involved in any research that the lecturers were doing.

Over the years I have been asked on many occasions what first got me involved in the alien big cat 'scene', and I used to answer that it was the China Fleet club sightings in 1994. In fact I have always had an interest in the concept of introduced species, and the possible environmental effects that they may have. I am also old enough to remember adverts in the weekly *Cage and Aviary Birds* from Tyseley Pet Stores, and others, for various exotic cats. So I suspect that I may have been thinking about the cause before the effect, so to speak.

The sighting of a large black cat at the China Fleet (golf) Club in 1994 bolstered my thoughts. There was some rubbish being spoken about the sighting, and some local 'experts' were regularly identifying dog footprints as belonging to big cats, blaming the Dangerous Wild Animals Act 1976 for the sightings. Both supplied easy answers and, to my mind, both were probably too easy, and therefore possibly erroneous. This suspicion lead me to get involved, and at least attempt and set the record straight.

The easiest way to do this was to try and get a letter in the local newspaper. The letter became an article, containing as it did far too much for a letter, and to my surprise they not only published the article, but turned up at my work to take an accompanying photograph. A walk around the golf course with the manager and a photographer friend led to a television interview and an analysis of some footprints found in the bunkers. The manager was very interested in the phenomena, and immediately declared the site to be a gun free zone. Interestingly, the groundsmen responded by saying that it wouldn't make any difference, as the rabbits had just about disappeared, although they had still been finding sets of severed back legs!

More sightings were reported to me directly from this site, many of which did not get into the press. I did, however, participate a television interview looking at footprints in the bunkers. As a result, I was suddenly inundated with offers for radio programme interviews and newspapers requests for comments on other sightings.

When the China Fleet sightings began to die down, I started to look at the archives in the local library and trying and work out when the first sightings of ABCs had occurred in the area. Interestingly, the Beast of Bodmin phenomenon was very much one of the 1990s, although there were alleged puma sightings further West in Cornwall as early as 1966.

South West Devon had sightings from 1966 onwards, often with gaps of several years but still predating the Beast of Exmoor, which effectively caught the attention of the media in the early 1980s. As such, South West Devon was possibly the area of greatest interest; it was only co-incidental that it was easily accessible, relatively unspoilt and quite beautiful.

The area that I picked to concentrate on was a polygon; effectively all to the South of Dartmoor and generally to the South of the A38, East of Plymouth, but South of a line drawn from Teignmouth due West to the A38. Occasionally I include sightings that stray North of the A38, where they only do so by a few miles and seem potentially contiguous with other sightings to the south of the A38. Because of the shape of the area and the somewhat arbitrary nature of the shape I refer to it as the South West Polygon (a sort of a logical progression from the "Bermuda Triangle").

This area includes two large and two small zoological collections that are open to the public, a third large collection (Plymouth Zoo) closed some time ago. There were also two other collections just outside the area that had, at various times, kept what would be now be called 'dangerous wild animals'. These were Exmouth Zoo, and a 'mini-zoo' at Launceston. Additionally, I am aware of rumours of one unlicensed person in the area keeping species listed in the Dangerous Wild Animal Act, although apparently not cats, and of one puma in private ownership in Paignton (pre-Act) in 1969.

Geographically the area is mainly South Devon countryside, not moorland, with many narrow roads and small villages. Most of the commonly used country walks tend to be coastal, and for that reason seasonal., and many of the river valleys are fairly steep sided and have been left as woodland.

For those who do not know the geography of the South West, the souths of the counties of Devon and Cornwall are separated by the river Tamar and any wild cat on the Cornish side of the river (which would include the China Fleet Club) could not get across into Devon without either crossing the river, or going some considerable distance inland. The animal sighted at the China Fleet club, however, would have had a range which was contiguous with the Bodmin Moor area, with no geographical barriers to block its Eastward movement until it got to the river Tamar. The logical conclusion, based mainly on timings and "black cat" descriptions, is that the animal sighted at the China Fleet club was in fact the offspring of the animal(s) living in the Bodmin Moor area which, when the time came for it to find its own range, headed East. Circumstantial evidence to link with this was the later sighting of a similar (black cat) animal at other locations north of the Golf Club.

Any animal in South Devon would almost certainly not have had its origins in Cornwall, unless it was either transported into South Devon, or came by a long and circuitous route though mid-Cornwall and mid/North Devon. In doing so it would have had to pass through large tracts of relatively wild country, much of which would have made suitable habitat.

The South Devon sightings really came into their own in the September of 1966, when the Holbeton area experienced a number of sightings of a Puma. Everyone is clear about what they saw; one local farmer even went to Plymouth Zoo to observe the panther there in order to confirm that it was a puma he saw. One of the local papers commented on the credibility of the sighting by pointing out that Commander Mildmay-White had seen the animal twice; it was the sixties and the word of an officer and a gentleman was not to be doubted! In 1967 there was also a report of a puma having been seen within the grounds of the Royal Naval Engineering College at Manadon in Plymouth. Although within the city, this was connected to the outskirts by a corridor of woods and countryside that is now the A38 (deer from the area still regularly enter the peripheries of the City).

The 1970s were relatively quiet, although a black animal with a small head was reported as being seen to the East of the City of Plymouth. This animal ran off at speed into the local woods.

The 1980s were again fairly quiet with a series of reports being focused mainly in 1983 and 1984. The 1983 reports were mainly concerned with a puma type animal in the Kingsbridge area. Multiple witnesses saw the animal, on separate occasions in the early evening, and at dusk. The 1984 sightings were around Modbury, Filham to the East of Ivybridge and Wrangaton, and were all of an animal that was jet-black, four times the size of a fox and moved like a cat. These sightings were taken seriously and the police helicopter was involved. A month later the *Kingsbridge Gazette* carried a picture of a Newfoundland Dog, who may have been mistaken for a big cat in two recent sightings (having been in the right place at the right time), although there were still numerous sightings that he could not have been responsible for. Despite this, there was a tendency for the Beast of Exmoor reports to overshadow everything else, and reports in the South of the county were quite likely ignored by all media besides the local papers.

Towards the end of the 1980s there was a clear sighting on the cliffs between Hallsands and Beesands. A couple from Bristol claimed to have got within twenty-five feet of a black panther that sat on the path in front of them, although the described white facial markings rather detracted from the otherwise panther like description. A month later another black cat was seen a few miles away at South Milton. The *Kingsbridge Gazette* picked up the stories, these villages being very much in their readership area, and a report of a large reddish-brown animal seen by a local farmer near South Milton was also carried. Nigel Brierly was interviewed in a later edition, and mentions of black pumas were carried in subsequent discussions.

The 1990s supplied a steadier stream of reports. 1990 started with a plea from Ellis Dawe, the owner of Dartmoor Wildlife Park, imploring people not to hunt pumas. This report came after a large cat claw had been recovered from a tree in Cornwall. In July of that year the *Kingsbridge Gazette* carried another report of a 'puma' sighting; unfortunately the description given was that of a black cat, which was initially mistaken for a black Labrador. As the two witnesses got closer though they decided that it was a cat. This sighting was at Higher Prawle. Later, in December of that year, Liz Montague of MGM Nurseries near Loddiswell and her father saw a large cat silhouetted on the skyline. This animal walked away when it heard them talking. Although there was a chicken missing they were reluctant to blame it on the cat.

1991 was quiet, but the second half of 1992 saw four ewes killed at Pennywell Farm near Buckfastleigh on consecutive nights, and a Labrador suffer life threatening injuries near its home in Bovey Tracey. The vet who operated on the Labrador stated that only a wire snare or a big cat could only have caused the injuries. A month later, towards the end of September, it was reported that a 16 year old girl had seen two large jet black cats a few miles from Widecombe about a month previously.

The following year Janice Comer saw a light coloured big cat near the entrance to the Holne Chase Hotel near Ashburton on a July evening. This report did not become public until the witness wrote a letter to the *Western Morning News* after MAFF published their report on the Beast of Bodmin in 1995.

Later in 1993 there was a large black cat seen on the Drumbridges to Newton Abbot road and 'puma-like' footprints seen at Broadhempston (nr. Totnes).

1994 passed without significant occurrences, but 1995 more than made up for it. As well as the Beast of Bodmin investigations in Cornwall there were big cat sightings from up and down the country, including some from areas where there were no previously recorded sightings. The South West Devon area started off in April with a puma sighting at the edge of Plymouth, in the suburbs of Plympton. The witness withheld their name, but the newspapers reported that there had been some 'pet slayings' in the area. The following day the local newspaper carried other reports of sightings from the Plympton area and from Langage (a little further to the East) where a grey-brown cat, bigger than a Springer Spaniel, was seen prowling the grounds of Westcountry TV (now ITV plc).

In June the South Devon and Plymouth Times reported a sighting of a large black animal running across the Totnes to Newton Abbot road, and then a week later the *Kingsbridge Gazette* reported another large black cat sighting at Aveton Gifford. Another report of a cat seen near Ivybridge in August this year didn't appear until 1999 when a book entitled "Stowford Paper Mill and the Industrial Heritage of the Erme Valley" was published; the author, Colin Harris, had seen an animal which he described as "darkish in colour, not jet black" at 9.05 pm one night in June 1995. His sketch shows a remarkably puma-like animal.

After the 1995 multiple sightings the newspaper reports reduced a little over the next few years. In 1996 a black cat was seen on the railway track at South Brent, yet despite the stated colour it was still referred to as a puma. In late 1997 Noela McKenzie saw a black cat near Bridgetown in Totnes "It was quite large and bigger than a domestic cat... its build was not that of a usual cat. It had long legs with a very long tail".

1998 was remarkable for the 'Wrangaton Lion' sightings. Wrangaton is about sixteen miles to the East of Plymouth and just North of the A38. It started on the 19th of November when Paul Gourley, who was driving East out of Wrangaton, saw a male lion with blood on its mane, run along a country lane and then jump through a hedge. At one stage he got within 20 metres of the animal. Just over an hour and a half later two workers claimed to have seen a big cat in a field three miles to the East of the first sighting. During the remainder of the morning a convoy of up to twenty vehicles charged around the local countryside. This included staff from the local zoo (it wasn't theirs), the media and the local police firearms unit. Nothing was found apart from some footprints, which the zoo staff identified as being those of a cat bigger than a puma.

The Following April (1999), again in the morning, two people were driving between Wrangaton and Bittaford when the driver saw a lion. He reversed to get a better look at it and the passenger then saw it too. She later described it as a "lion or a puma". Again the force firearms unit attended, this time with a helicopter and thermal imaging equipment. Using the imaging equipment an animal was located, by thermal image only, in dense woodland, but then disappeared. When the officers on the ground were directed to where the image had disappeared they found themselves in the middle of an active badger set. The film was shown on television that night with an 'expert' present. She couldn't decide what it was, but to my eyes it was remarkably badger like!

Over the next few days more sightings occurred, many closer to Ivybridge, and the County Council issued a warning to parents suggesting that small children in the area be accompanied to and from school. A few days after this a local lady wrote a letter to the newspaper suggesting that the sightings might have been of her golden retriever, who had previously been mistaken for a lion.

1998 saw the reports of puma-like cats continue, with a report from Washbourne and one from near California Cross. Although the lions sightings caused a greater distraction than the smaller black cat sightings, there was yet another black cat sighting at Cornwood, North of the A38 in October 1999.

Early 2000 led to a report of a big black cat seen near the A38 by the turn off for Chudleigh. That was about the only report from within this area for 2000.

In October 2001 another big black cat report came in from the A38, this time sighted at the turn off at Ugborough.

Initially more interesting was the videotape that was brought in to a local newspaper in September 2001. A couple who had been holidaying at the Bigbury Holiday Park had seen a couple of big black cats each year for the past five years; having finally videoed them they went to a local newspaper. The paper contacted Paul Crowther and myself and we both had a look at it. Sadly it showed two mature black domestic cats. This was a disappointment for the paper, and presumably for the couple who had filmed them.

2003 brought the odd sighting, but nothing of great note except for a possible horse attack in August. This occurred in a field bordering on the A38 at South Brent. At the behest of the British Big Cat Society, with which I was still involved at the time, I examined the horse and the field where the attack was alleged to have taken place. The local police attended as well, and I was asked if I thought that the horse had been 'interfered' with. I passed on that one, saying that was definitely one for the vet. The injuries to the horse could have been done by a big cat, but if so it had been a half-hearted attack and the cat may possibly have been injured.

2004 didn't see many reports of sightings until October, when there were a se-ries of reports of a mystery cat from the Plymouth area. The witnesses con-cerned though it to be an Ocelot on one occasion and a Serval on another. When I discussed it with the reporter concerned, and showed him pictures of a Bengal (domestic) cat, it was agreed that this was probably what had been seen. A few reports from 2003 also came into the paper at this point when the 'spotty cat' stories were published. This story stretched over into January 2005 with foot-prints found in the Heybrook Bay area. They were going up a wall, and at a height and size that was incompatible with a domestic cat. Unfortunately these footprints were too small to be that of a leopard or puma, so I went again for the Bengal as an obvious explanation. A week later a local Bengal cat was photo-graphed and featured with its owner in the paper. At this stage an eyewitness had come forward, but she was of the opinion that the pictured Bengal was smaller than the animal that she had seen.

The spotty cat reports then stopped and I received a report from Alan White, via the British Big Cat Research Group (BBCRG), of a sighting of what was ini-tially thought to be a puma. This had occurred in early January on the North side of the river Dart. The initial witness, who had been out walking his dog, con-tacted Alan after looking at some books. Two people in the area subsequently went hunting for it, and saw what they said was a puma running away from them. The identification was on the basis of having previously seen pumas, and the animal's movement, gait and tail.

In June another sighting was reported, indirectly through a BBCRG member. This time it was a black animal, near Ashburton, but South of the A38. A wit-ness who had seen German Shepherd dogs in the same location saw the animal in a field from 60 – 70 feet. This animal was described as large, in comparison to the dogs. The animal was described as dark, not black, and as having a small head. It cleared the field quickly, but retraced its steps, crossing the field in the opposite direction a few minutes later.

June also saw an attack on a cow at Langage farm. The injuries to the animal's face, and the pattern and speed of infliction were very consistent with a preda-tor, possibly not used to prey of this size, having seized it by the mouth. At an interview arranged by Chris Johnston the manager of the farm said that two of his workers had, some time previous to the attack, seen a large black cat on the periphery of the farm. The second report of this incident also carried a report of a 'giant black cat' being seen at St. Anne's Chapel (less than ten miles South of Langage).

A black cat then appeared just behind a stone wall at a house on the Eastern edge of Ivybridge at about 5.00pm on the 11th of July. I was able to interview the witness 24 hours later and place a cut-out puma-sized cat in the same posi-tion. The witness was very credible and very pleased to have seen what he saw. Interestingly, he had also seen a large black cat a few years previously near the

Ivybridge Rugby club. These sightings are both contiguous with areas of other sightings, and of at least one suspicious sheep kill.

In August a reporter on a local newspaper contacted me about a sighting the previous night by a friend of his. She had sighted an animal the previous night in the California Cross/Loddiswell area. As she was more than happy to meet me at the site I attended, again with the cut out, that afternoon. The site was a field entrance on the road. The gate leading into the field was open and across the valley there was a farm, where the dogs had recently been given to bouts of inexplicable barking at night. The lady confirmed the size with the cut out. She had originally stated that the animal was the size of a Great Dane, but she later confessed to having possibly exaggerated; it was the only dog breed that she could think of at the time that was bigger than a Collie!

This lady was very pleased to have seen the animal, and was fed up that her friend who was desperate to see one had not been with her. Interestingly, several of her other friends had seen big cats in the area over the last few years, but none had ever reported the sightings. Their reasons for not making statements ranged from fear of ridicule and fear of unnecessary publicity, to concerns for the animals' safety.

Ten days later I was back in the same area looking at a dead sheep. It had been killed by a predator and it's head had been removed. The animal was freshly killed, and I believe that the owners may have disturbed the predator when they discovered the body at 7.00 am. The owners wished to remain anonymous, having previously received some adverse comments when they reported seeing a large black cat in the area. Their two dogs (a large but friendly breed) will not leave the house on some nights.

On the way back into Plymouth I stopped at the California Cross pub and overheard a discussion about a local farmer who had just shot a fox taking his chickens. He had apparently been initially hesitant to shoot, thinking the animal was the cat which regularly passes through his property!

OVERVIEW AND CONCLUSIONS

Until recently I had been mainly investigating this area by collecting newspaper reports and other second hand data. In the last six months I have been going out into the field more, as a result of which I have, not surprisingly, made more contacts and have a better idea of what is actually happening out there. By making friends with several local newspaper reporters I have also confirmed that they sometimes get reports which are not published, due to either excess of current stories and space being at a premium, or to other big cat stories from different parts of the county are being carried.

Irregularity can also been seen in the incidence of reports arriving at the newspaper offices. We know that following the arrival of the police fire-arms unit at the 'Wrangaton Lion' sightings, a number of reports were withheld by witnesses because they were concerned for the animals safety. The foot and mouth epizootic in 2001 also restricted the number of people driving around the countryside, and therefore the potential for sightings. Additionally, no landowner with livestock was going to do or say anything that might attract people on to their land.

The region does show an interesting pattern of sightings that would suggest a breeding population of exotic cats of possibly two types. Pumas would appear to have been sighted since 1966 to the current day, with the occasional gap of a year or two. This is fairly consistent with the patterns that we see in those States of America where the animal is officially extinct, but still occasionally seen. Many of the sightings have specific claims that the animal seen was a puma, although some them refer to it being black in colour. The general description of a dark brown, or brown, cat-like animal with a long tail is also regularly given where the animal could not be any other known species.

The black cat situation is somewhat more complex; many professional zoologists find it hard to accept that leopards could survive here, whilst accepting that pumas and lynx could. Whilst I find it difficult to say with certainty that these animals do exist here, I am aware that some of the descriptions could practically be little else. I am also aware of leopards existing in parts of Africa and Asia where they were previously thought to be extinct. In these countries they are often found up to the edges of cities where the population are, in the main, unaware of them.

We certainly have large domestic feral cats in this area. For some reason that, as far as I am aware, is unknown, domestic cats (particularly ones black in colour) are often alleged to grow to be larger in the wild than when living in domesticity. There was also a report, early in 2005, of a large domestic cat stalking and attacking lambs in New Zealand.

It is also possible that a 'Kellas' type hybrid exists here. A Kellas type hybrid is one that resulted from a domestic cat crossing with a European (Scottish) Wildcat. It is, however, far from clear when the European Wildcat died out in the South West. According to Derek Yalden's book *The History of British Mammals* (1999), it would appear to be before 1800. This does seem a little premature, and, as hybridisation with domestic cats seems possible, even if that date was correct, there may still be wildcat genes present in some modern cats. These would, however, be much diluted.

Whatever the species, there are undoubtedly large wild black cats being seen and reported regularly in the study area since 1970. Some of these have been described as pumas, almost certainly erroneously. They are also occasionally described as having small heads, a feature apparent in some of the descriptions of Kellas cats before they were properly depicted. To some extent it might be expected that if the animals were (black) leopards their heads would be described as large, or at least not be conspicuously small in relation to the rest of the body.

The spotty cats that were sighted in 2004-2005 were almost certainly Bengals, a domestic cat breed produced by hybridising the Domestic Cat with the Leopard Cat. They have been becoming increasingly popular as pets because of their size, colouring and temperament. Although smaller cats such as Servals, Leopard Cats and Ocelots could almost certainly survive here, there are no suggestions of any being loose in this area except for the Leopard Cat that was shot near Widdecombe in 1988. Even this animal was only thought to have been loose for a few weeks.

In the case of the Bengal cat I am concerned that because of the wild genes within them (some are F2 and F3 generations and so would contain 25% and 12.5% Leopard Cat genes respectively) they may be well suited to a life as feral cats and could become established with apparent ease. There is some limited evidence to suggest that this might already be happening in Lancashire.

The situation in this area is, as it is in the rest of the country, very fluid. However, when the records are studied, a pattern does seem to be beginning to develop. These patterns do indicate certain areas where sightings of exotic cats, or evidence of them, recurs. These areas are not inconsistent with those that might be selected by a large exotic predator seeking a home range in a new territory.

FUTURE WORK

As such this area will continue to be studied and, as the appropriate evidence appears, it will be investigated. Additionally, further newspaper searches will be made; particularly for the periods 1966 – 1980. This period is a particularly difficult one to research because the newspapers are not typically recorded on a searchable database system and neither were there any researchers keeping detailed archives on this subject area. Also any report that appeared in a local newspaper was likely to stay in that newspaper, and not be carried by the nationals. Investigation into, as yet unsubstantiated, allegations of releases of animals into this and surrounding areas will also continue.

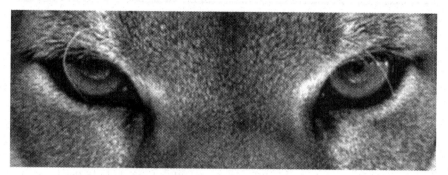

Argyll Big Cats 2005
by Shaun Stevens

- *Shaun - now nearing his fortieth year - has been interested in unexplained phenomena from the age of ten. With a great love of mystery animals, and cryptozoology in general, he was glad to find that when he moved to Argyll there was a big cat practically on his doorstep.*

So here I am, sitting at the keyboard, trying to put into words my first year of involvement with the BCIB research group.

It has been a very interesting and informative time and, although I've yet to meet any of the group in person, the continual movement of emails across the internet makes me feel part of a dedicated group of people determined to get that all important piece of evidence - that piece of evidence which will finally prove to all those sceptics that Big Cats are not only out there, but thriving in the wilds of Britain.

Even though most sightings may be of imported cats, we shouldn't forget our own native cats. We all know of the Scottish Wildcat, a beautiful animal, and we were lucky enough this year to get not only a confirmed sighting in the area, but actual video footage as well (more of that later). There is also the extremely rare Kellas Cat, a creature which inspires hot debate as to whether or not it is also a native species.

The region of Argyll, including the peninsulas of Cowal and Kintyre, have had regular sightings of big cats over the years; not surprising considering the huge tracts of forests and moorlands in the area. Situated on the West coast of Scotland, with the gulf stream ensuring mild winters and warm summers, the area is a haven for wildlife. Deer, foxes, badgers, otters, polecats, mink and wild goats are regularly seen. (I'm even convinced that I once saw a red squirrel about 12 years ago in mid Argyll, even though they are not supposed to exist now in the region). An abundance of game birds including pheasant and grouse also inhabit the local shoreline here in Campbeltown, as do the common rabbit and not so common hare, numerous swans, ducks, geese, oyster catchers, cormorants and two herons named "Harry" and "Harriet". Buzzards hover and circle over the hills and fields, and the early evening is a prime time to see several species of owls sitting on the telegraph poles. Several years ago I witnessed a pair of peregrine falcons swooping down from the top of the church in Campbeltown, unfortunately they only stayed a week or so. As dusk falls, bats swoop over your head, which can be a bit of a nightmare when you are trying to walk three dogs and they are all trying to catch the bats as they flit overhead.

And then we have the grey and common seals that I see daily in the loch, although if I had my way they wouldn't be so common. These local aquatic residents have learnt that if you wait by the pier when someone is fishing, someone will catch the fish for you. It's a race to reel the fish in before the seals catch up with you. Then it's a game of tug and war between you and the seal. It's a common occurence to be left with only a head at the end of the contest. My son and I have lost many fish, hooks and lines to these greedy little *!&@$@!*: (only kidding really, watching these creatures from a distance of a couple of metres, twisting and turning in the water can be a joy to watch. I just wish they'd leave my fish alone.........)

And if all that wildlife is not enough for anybody, we can now definitely add wildcats to the list.

So you can see, we are very lucky, in that not only have we an abundance of local wildlife, but we also have our 'cats'. This year an article in my local paper *The Campbeltown Courier* made mention of not only a possible sighting of a wildcat in the area, but the existence of video footage as well. According to 'Wildcat' experts (I won't mention their names but they claim to be the leading experts on the species) this was something that was impossible, because in their words "wildcats are not found that far South". A follow up just had to be done, so I made arrangements to meet a Mr and Mrs Bakes at their home on Wednesday 15th June 2005. Below is a copy of the report I made to the group.

"After speaking with them it appears that several neighbours have seen the cat on numerous occasions since the beginning of the year. Only two weeks ago two tourists nearly ran over a "large black cat", just outside the entrance to their home. A neighbours' elderly cat has also disappeared recently.

They have regularly seen paw prints and spoors and heard screeching at night. They are going to film and photograph any future sightings for us, and wherever possible take casts and photos of any prints.

Both the gentleman and lady are keen naturalists. The lady, being a member of a badger watch at a previous address. The have seen otters, mink, fox and roe deer on their land and in the river that flows in the small valley beside their house.

They have also spotted rare butterflies. So I feel that they are excellent, knowledgeable witnesses.

The sighting was made about 5am from an upstairs window. They watched the cat for about 5 minutes before thinking about video recording it. In the video you first see the cat from distance before he zooms in the camera. The path the cat walks up is about 2 foot across.

The cat stops at a step, which measures 8 inches high. The cat spots a mouse or vole run across the path (probably a vole because the couple say there are lots of voles in the bank there) and bounds after it. The cat covers the distance between two steps in two bounds. The distance between the steps is just over 6 foot.

The cat then jumps into the long grass after the vole. The grass was about 2 foot high at the time, and you can see the striped tail clearly waving about. They have a very large pet cat themselves, which measures about 12 inches at the shoulder. Taking all these measurements into consideration, I estimate the cat to be about 18 inches high and a body length of about 30 inches. About one and a half times the size of their very large cat.

From the size and the markings I have no doubt that it is a Scottish Wild Cat. The cat has the distinctive striped tail, dark stripe down its back and smallish head compared to its body. All of which are distinctive characteristics of the wild cat."

Hopefully, in the near future, we shall be able to get this extremely rare footage onto the website, for everyone to enjoy.

That, to me, was the highlight of cat sightings during 2005 in Argyll. However, its bigger cousins didn't let us down; although sightings were a little down this year, they did put in an appearance. Most sightings appear to coincide with the winter months. This may be possibly due to the cats having difficulty finding food and shelter in the winter months and encroaching on areas closer to human habitation and farmland.

There appears to have been several hotspots for sightings in the region over the last year.

Down in the south of Kintyre we had numerous sightings of a black cat, including one by my father-in-law. (how jealous am I....?) .There were also a couple of sightings of a brown lynx type cat. This brown cat appears to have been seen only during the last few years, which makes me think we have had an animal released into the area.

In Mid-Kintyre, a black cat has been seen in the Clachan area.

Other hotspots include Dunoon, in the Cowal peninisular, and the area around Oban in the North. The majority of sightings have been of the usual 'black' variety.

Unlike many of the group, I've yet to see my first big cat. However, as soon as my work commitments allow, I'll be joining the group on one of the vigils. I will be expecting the group to not let me down, and to do their best, in ensuring I see one of the elusive beasts. Fingers crossed of course. Until then, I'll have to restrict my involvement in the group to doing my daily news search on the internet for big cat news and doing follow-ups on local sightings.

Still, I may not get to see any big cats, but there is plenty of other wildlife to keep me going.

I'm off now, to have an argument with a seal. I'll probably lose…again!

Gloucestershire Big Cats
by Trystan Swale

• *Trystan Swale is a researcher for the Gloucestershire based Severnside Centre for Fortean Research. His main interests are cryptzoology, earth mysteries and the study of ghostly animals (zooform phenomena).*

Summer is often silly season in the truest sense of the words, as the powers that be take annual leave, but in Gloucestershire during 2005 we've been treated to a number of ABC (alien big cat) sightings in the local press.

March saw a West Oxfordshire farming community draw national attention with its hunt for a 'large black cat' subsequently dubbed 'the beast of Burford'. Even the local wildlife park got in on the action, offering a reward for the capture of the beast. Predictably, nobody has yet to get a grip on the beast, however reports in the local press have suggested a glut of sightings drifting a long way to the West. Whilst we're not suggesting that the Burford behemoth is the one and the same cause of the initial sightings, May saw sightings of at least one ABC in the Cheltenham area of Gloucestershire. *The Gloucestershire Echo* of 11 May carried the story with an oh-so-predictable headline 'people with big cat tails to tell':

"A Big black cat has been spotted wandering around Woodmancote and Leckhampton. Witnesses have described a cat, at least a metre in length, with a small head and long tail. The Echo reported that Hucclecote pensioners Mary and Jim Alison believed a big cat had decapitated their tabby Tigger. Big cat tracker Frank Tunbridge, from Podsmead, said he had received several calls. He said: "There's been sightings of a big black cat in Woodmancote, Badgeworth and Leckhampton. All of them give the same description. It's probably the same cat. These animals cover a huge area. The most recent was about a week ago but some of the sightings date back to last year."

John Blenkinsop, who lives in Woodmancote, said he had seen the beast. The

70-year-old was walking along Stockwell Lane towards Cleeve Hill at 7pm when he noticed something moving on a footpath to his right. He said: "It looked like a cat, only much bigger. It was about 3ft high. It slinked past a fence and then disappeared. I was walking up Cleeve Hill when I passed the field full of sheep."

Other witnesses claim to have seen a big black cat chasing deer in Badgeworth and crossing the road on Leckhampton Hill. Mr Tunbridge, who has been tracking big cats since the 1970s, believes there are about 500 roaming the British countryside; the result of pets being released into the wild. He said: "During the 1960s and 70s it was fashionable to keep exotic animals. But in 1976 when the Dangerous Wild Animals Act came into force, people released their cats rather than pay for a licence."

By June 1 the letters page of *The Gloucestershire Echo* had featured a number of other pieces of correspondence from readers claiming to have seen an ABC. One anonymous correspondent wrote "I am yet another reader who has spotted a big cat in the area. In fact, I have seen one twice. The first time was when I was out riding my horse very early in the morning on the far side of Cleeve Hill. At first I thought it was a deer or something but as I got closer I realised with amazement it was a huge black cat the size of a panther. The second time was only a few months ago, again when I was out riding. This time the people I was with saw it as well, and were also flabbergasted. This sighting was on Stanley Mount, which are the woods above Gotherington and Gretton. When I have told other local people about seeing a big cat I have been amazed at how much evidence there is. Other people have seen one and gamekeepers have reported lambs being mauled." (Letters, May 19)

STROUD SIGHTINGS

As the area to the north of Cheltenham wrestled with its own big black cat, both the Cirencester and Stroud areas in the south of the county began to chronicle sightings - yet again suggesting that there could be more than one big cat on the loose. *The Stroud News and Journal*, June 4, reported: "A chance sighting at the weekend has added credibility to police claims that big cats are at large in the Five Valleys. Last week wildlife liaison officer Mark Robson said there was just too much evidence to dismiss the existence of jet-black leopards roaming wild."

Minchinhampton taxi driver George Hearn is backing the animal officer after watching a black beast glide across the road in front of his cab. "I was driving back to Minchinhampton at about 12.30am on Friday night," he said. "And this cat glided across the road in front of me." Mr Hearn said he had no doubt about what he had seen and, as a taxi driver often using the roads at unsociable hours, he has plenty of experience of seeing wildlife dart across the beam of his headlights. "It moved far too fast to be a dog and it certainly wasn't a deer," he said.

"It didn't stop to glare at me, it just glided across the road and disappeared into the hedge. It was jet black with no markings and it was quick. I'm certain it was a black cat of some sort. If I'd been going much faster I'd have hit it for sure."

The beast, which was spotted on the road between Aston Down and the *Ragged Cot Inn* [ironically, just off the main Stroud to Cirencester road - SCFR], was about the size of a Labrador dog. Mr Hearn said he believed there had been so few sightings because the exotic animals only tend to be out on the prowl when most of us are tucked up in bed. "They are definitely out there," he said. "I suppose I'd believed the other people who said they had seen them but I hadn't taken much notice until I saw one myself.'"

CIRENCESTER AREA ABCS

By June 2 big cat sightings had spread towards and into the suburbs of Cirencester. *The Wilts. and Gloucestershire Standard* of that date reported: "A big cat specialist is on his way to the Cotswolds after scores of sightings in the Cirencester area. Danny Bamping, founder of the British Big Cat Society says he has received so many reports of big cat sightings in the Cirencester area he is now planning to carry out an expedition to the area in an attempt to gain hard evidence. In the most recent sighting on Sunday evening, Watermoor resident Pauline Saunders saw a feline creature the size of a dog prowling the street. Pauline Saunders, who lives in Kingsmead, had just seen her postman son off to work when she caught sight of the mysterious creature. Through her half-opened door she watched it stroll along a row of cars under the light of street lamps before disappearing into the darkness. Pauline said: "It came from under a car over the road and was at least four times the size of a normal domestic cat. I was watching it with the door open a bit. It just sauntered down the middle of the road as if it didn't care where it was. We have lots of cats down here and we see foxes occasionally but this was black and much bigger."

Recently the subject of big cats has been one of hot debate, following a series of sightings across the country, even in London. Pauline added: "It wasn't quite as big as a panther but at least four times the size of a cat. It was quite frightening - it gave me goose-pimples." The BBCS has been processing scores of sightings of unusual feline creatures in the Cotswolds.

Danny Bamping said: "I know the Watermoor area quite well because we have had quite a few sightings around that place. Cirencester borders on greener pastures, expansive fields and streams - if the cats get hungry they will take any opportunity to scavenge. But these cats can do 25-30 kilometres on one night if they want to so it can be quite difficult to keep track of them. We always look closely at all the data and many aren't genuine sightings, but there are still hundreds of people who undoubtedly see these animals. The Cotswolds is perfect for them and I hope to come down in the late summer.'"

HIGH PROFILE WITNESS

In its edition of June 30 the *Wilts and Gloucestershire Standard* appeared to give weight to the sightings, stating that the chief executive of the local district council had reported his own encounter: 'The creature was prowling near children's playing fields on the corner of Grange Court. Stratton has a lot of green open space adjacent to residential property, exactly the kind of location where previous sightings have occurred." Mr Austin said: "I am absolutely certain about what I saw. It was about the size of a Labrador but definitely not a domestic cat or dog. It was about 75 yards away and this cat-like animal was right on the corner of Grange Court and the open play area. It was standing absolutely still with an arched back and for a moment I thought it might have been a prank, but then it dropped its back, turned in a circle and walked towards the primary school. I didn't follow it because it was bigger the my dog and thought it wouldn't be a good idea - it was about two feet high and four feet long, with a thick tail." Mr Austin said he had just read a report in last week's Standard about more sightings before going out for a walk that morning. Since the story was published, the newsroom received several calls from residents with similar stories. Mr Austin said: "I suppose I was surprised but having just read the article in the Standard I probably took more notice. I wasn't particularly frightened because I have been around animals all my life - it didn't make any threatening moves or anything. It just looked king of the patch and not at all worried about people.'"

ABC fever maintained its grip over the local press, and as Cirencester continued to have its own share of reports (hindered by a rather crude hoax with supposed paw prints appearing on the Standard editor's car) Stroud was not to be left behind. The July 20th edition of the *Stroud News and Journal* ran a small feature on big cats in the district which featured news of yet more sightings, although many were unsubstantiated. However, more convincing was this tale:

Retired policeman Roy Harvey, 73, from Amberley, believes he spotted what looked like a black panther in his garden early one morning. He said: "You occasionally see these reports in the paper about people spotting large cats and I had always read them with a degree of cynicism, until I saw a large cat - the size of a big fox - in our garden. I watched it for about two minutes until it disappeared. It was a lot bigger than your average domestic cat with dark brown to black fur."

There have been other rumoured sightings of large cats around the Five Valleys in Rodborough, Woodchester, Minchinhampton, Nailsworth and Nymphsfield as well as in nearby Cirencester. Mr Harvey said he couldn't believe his eyes when he saw it. He added: "I'd never seen anything like that in my life. I was a policeman for 25 years and saw plenty of foxes and badgers while on night duty, but this was different."

In August things seemed to go quiet in Stroud and Cirencester, so it was perhaps not surprising to see tales of big cats emerging to the south in the Dursley area of the county.

From the *Gazette* of 26 August:

"A Wickwar farmer has one of his prized pedigree sheep savaged by what is believed to be a big cat. John Terrett arrived at his farm, on the outskirts of the village, last Wednesday morning to find the remains of one of his Jacob sheep lying on the ground surrounded by its fleece. The nine-month-old sheep had been due to be sold at market when it was killed.

Mr Terrett told the *Gazette* this week that none of the other sheep in his pedigree accredited flock, which he keeps at Osbournes Farm, were attacked and there had been no signs there was a big cat in the area. "We believe that this was done by a big cat in the hours of darkness." This has been confirmed by DEFRA and a big cat specialist. "There have been no paw prints to suggest a big cat has been here. We had a look around the farm but we didn't see any paw marks on the ground. It is a shame that the ground wasn't softer because then we could have seen its paw marks. All we have got left of the animal is bones - the skull, backbone, rib cage, pelvis and front legs. We have been told that if it was a dog, fox or badger that did this they would have left teeth marks but we are told that big cats lick the meat off the bones and don't chew so they don't leave marks. "Nobody seems to know about the big cat and the specialist said hopefully it is a one-off attack."

It is not the first time that Mr Terrett, who lives at Cromhall, has come across a big cat in the area. "I have seen a big cat before about four or five years ago and it has been seen by a local game keeper," he said. "My sons and I also saw a big cat crossing the road two years ago at Christmas."

Cats, Tracks and Trials
by Alan White

• *I was born on the Island of Jersey in the Channel Islands, and have been interested in all aspects of Wildlife since a very early age. Living close to Jersey Zoo, and its Big Cats section, was an inspiration. I have been lucky to have seen most of the World's Big cats in their natural and native habitats, and so it was with added pleasure and surprise that in 1979 I saw my first big cat in the UK, in Wales; it was a Lynx.*

I arrived in the Torbay area in 1981. I lived in Paignton, a long stone's throw away from Paignton Zoo and the surrounding Clennon Valley Woods. Little did I know that before very long I would know practically know every inch of them. Taking the bus to work in Brixham every day, I got to know many of the locals in the higher Brixham area. This was mainly during my lunch hour in the Waterman's Arms in St Mary's square. I felt these visits constituted a good way of getting to know the locals as well as having a good time into the bargain. It was on one of these research laden visits that I overheard one of the local tradesmen talking of a large sandy coloured cat, which had been seen in the grounds of Collaton Fishacre. I casually asked where this actually was; "On the way to Kingswear" my bar-hugging friend replied. Making a mental note to find out more about the area, I continued listening as the electrician told everyone around him about the cat. He adjusted his voice to a more dramatic tone and said in quieter tones (or so he thought; in truth everyone in the bar could hear him) that the cat "had been seen by the gardeners in broad daylight".

My senses came alive to this snippet of info and I thought back to 1979 when I had seen and heard two Lynx in an area of South Wales. I had to pinch myself somewhat to believe that what I was hearing was true. I also thought that maybe this was just local gossip, about something which may have in reality been a domestic moggy. I got to know these stories over the years. "Man eating Panther at Large" had been one of the headlines in the older sixties tabloids. It had always amused me that a man would eat a panther…what part would he eat first?.

I made a note of this so I could ask John about it the next time he came in for petrol; that is, about the Collaton Cat and not how a man would eat a panther. When I returned from my liquid lunch I spoke to my work colleague Sam about what had been said. "Oh that" he remarked nonchalantly, "There's been a lot of sightings over the last few years, especially in and around the areas between here and Kingswear". He paused for a second and passed me the car polish. "You should go out and about sometime, who knows what you might find". When I got to know Sam I realised that this comment may certainly have had a double meaning, one which I found out much later when bird watching around Scabbacombe point. The area he was referring to turned out to be a naturist beach. 'Nuff said.

The whole of the Brixham and Kingswear peninsular is covered by coastal foot-paths which run all along the eastern side of the coast before deviating to the other side at Kingswear, up along the River Dart and eventually leading towards Totnes. There are many different valleys and gullies along the seaward coast, all covered by many different types of vegetation which are unique to the local soils and climate. Many of the deep areas seem to be inaccessible when it comes to the possibility of humans invading their privacy. Climbing equipment may well be needed for the descents. The coastal paths are used by the diehard walk-ers in all weathers, but for the uninitiated they're like a fairground ride. I quickly learnt that I would need decent footwear, and I was taught more than once not to take the area for granted when it came to being safety conscious. Once I was fitted out with everything I needed to survive; drink, food, notebook, etc., I set out into the wild blue yonder. It was while I was out that my ideas about the search for the cats took on a new angle. I began to look for clues just as a policeman would at a crime scene. Just thinking about this brought a whole new angle to my views on searching for evidence, and in turn to my expecta-tions of what I might find in doing so.

Apart from searching out in the actual field I spent a lot of time in the local li-brary, painstakingly going over books and maps that might help me. Yes, "Right Miss, can you help me" I thought of asking the assistant. "I am looking for a book that will help me track down any big cats within the South Devon area. What category would that be under?" The answer may well have been "Loonies down to the back of the library please, and wait amongst the self help books. Someone will attend to you when the men with white van and coats to match arrive."

Luckily I did not have this problem, and I soon found a lot of info gleaned by people working in other countries with many of the big cats, which did help a lot. They led me further and closer to learning about the behaviour of many of the large cats. The local maps and history of the area also provided endless knowledge, which in future months would help me in my movements around the peninsular.

Through basic knowledge of wildlife watching and orienteering I began making my own maps to go with the maps, which became essential for quick and easy reference when out in the field. Along with that I mounted a plan of campaign that linked with the seasons. If sailors needed the skies to move around, then why shouldn't I do the same on terra firma? Taking notes on the behaviour of the indigenous wildlife was a must. If I could learn their patterns, then I could hopefully figure out if and when they were behaving in a strange manner.

In planning this I also tried to imagine myself in these different scenarios. What would be the fastest point between A and B? How could I get from one place to another within a specific time limit? It was from this idea that I found more paths inland that were mapped, and also some that were not. This became essential for me at this time, as I still was using Shank's pony to get about.

At first I never really approached any of the locals directly, although being a birdwatcher and having a general interest in all aspects of nature certainly helped to break down barriers. I met a fellow wildlife watcher who turned out to be a postman - here was a man who knew a lot of people, and the fact that he loved mammals of all sizes helped. Over the next few years, Colin became a valuable source of knowledge as to what was going on, or what was not as the case sometimes was. He also got to see more animal road kills than I think any-one has ever seen. It was Colin who began to tell me who was who in the area, and their views on any local wildlife. Also, he told me who was approachable, and who was not. The farms, stables, and anywhere that kept cattle, sheep, horses, poultry, etc. became 'X marks the spot' areas for possible easy prey categories. Many of these people I learnt came into the garage anyway; these customers were singled out for the car and vehicle valeting flyers I was handing out. I was certainly lucky that any of them employed me, as it also helped me to learn the lie of their land.

It also occurred to me after a conversation with a keeper at Paignton Zoo that the people in this part of the country tended to keep quite a few exotic pets. This later became more evident than I would have ever thought. He also told me that if a certain animal has been kept caged, whether that animal was still living there or not, the scent would linger on for some time after.

All of the property boundaries; walls, hedges, whatever they were, became possibilities for future vantage points, not only for me but also for the cats, according to what height they were and where they were positioned.

A lot of the deep gorges and valleys along the coastal areas have a lot of low lying scrub and pasture, and plenty of rabbits. I likened this to a 'Roman arena' for the cats, full of food just ready for the taking. As the years went by the vegetation on these sites began to be controlled by goats, and with some success; although a few did become 'food on the hoof'.

One valley which had a lot of open area was that at Mansands. This was very close to Woodhuish, which had paths and bridleways for the horse riders. From these lanes the area falls down into a vast open area of marshland. In all seasons there are always plenty of Wildfowl and many other birds. This became a brilliant stamping ground for me and, I hoped, the cats. I had been told on many occasions that dead wildfowl had been found in the area. I knew that foxes could be amongst the main predators, but hoped that there might just be other predators to consider. There was a possibility that a cat might see this area as a vast, accessible food platter.

Access to this area and to the beach was either down a steep slope, or via a very rocky track which only a high wheel-base motor could manage. Consequently, on many occasions I found myself taking the steep slope of the coastal path. Coming down this, I likened it to a parachute jump without the parachute. However, after the first few descents in the dry, I began to get used to it. But when the wet weather set in, well…we all know the saying "the bigger they are the harder they fall".

Coming up to my first 4 or 5 months of working in Brixham, and living there as well, I began to find the locals less restless and more friendly. I began to gain confidence with the people coming into the garage. The word was getting around that I was just not a weird Channel Islander; slowly yet surely people were beginning to talk. Some told stories that had been handed down over the years. I learnt quite a lot, not just about cats in the surrounding area, but also about those sighted towards the outlying country, outwards and up to the Dartmoor edges. One lady told me of a time when she had been walking her dog on the bridleway at Woodhuish, and had been startled by a big black cat that had crossed the path and headed into the valley that lead to Mansands. I asked her if she could tell me which direction it had come from. "I'll do better than that" she told me, "I'll show you tomorrow." The next day she showed me the fields, which were close to the local riding stables just over the hill. She also told me that people's animals had been becoming more skittish in the Spring time. I thanked her and went up the bridle way towards the stables.

"Bull by the horns time" I told myself, "but be polite". I approached the stables and gathered immediately from the noise that they kept ducks. I was soon talking to the owner, who seemed to have a sixth sense in sensing that there was someone on their property. I by-passed a lot of the pleasantries and asked if she had lost any of her ducks. She told me that the birds had been disappearing at intervals, and that they had also heard noises both at night and in the early morning. I asked if they knew what it might me, but she did not answer. I left it at that, but did ask her to phone me if any more ducks or livestock went missing or were spooked. In the coming months the stables became a regular haunt, and the owners were always very willing to come and pick me up. I sat up outside on many occasions, but all that was said by the owner was "seems like we missed the offender yet again." Although I was in my element, the plain truth of it was that the darn creature seemed to be playing hide and seek with us. I am sure that one morning I even heard a hearty cat-like laugh resounding from a nearby thicket.

My walks were also becoming more and more frequent. Not always regimented, as they were in the beginning, but at all odd times of the day and the night. Once I got stopped by the local police whilst out wandering and they invited me into their car. They knew who I was and what I was doing, and were quite willing to provide shelter. I secretly think that they were glad to get away from their regular patrols and from some of the humdrum chores of night duty. It was from these beginnings that many years later the constables came up trumps for me, after a phone call from a late night dog walker, but that's for another report.

It was the morning after one of these walks that the local vet came into the garage for petrol with his Landrover and horse box. I began to fill it up as usual. The man began to talk. "Bloody foxes had one of my foals last night", he said. I nearly replied "well, if you leave them out what do you expect?", however I was glad I did not. Instead I asked where it had happened. "The field bordering the school valley" came the reply, an area just a few minutes up the road from where I now live. He continued talking and gestured towards the horsebox. "The carcass is in the back" he said, "do you want to take a look?" I put the fuel nozzle back into the pump "Alright" I said, and followed him to the rear of the box and the upright ramp. I looked into the box and my eyes adjusted to the low light. As soon as I saw the state of the foal, I told him immediately that a fox did not cause the damage. The neck and the shoulder area had been well and truly clawed. There were more marks on the body and the neck, and the area below had been opened up. "I've got a good idea what did this" I told him. He replied that he had thought I would like to see it before he disposed of it.

I cottoned on that he may have known just a little more about how and where I was spending my spare time. He continued speaking. "One of my lads heard a rasping and a screeching noise last night and went out to the field," he smiled at me. "You're very welcome to come and sit in the field at any time you want," he told me. I nodded enthusiastically, trying not to look too much like an automated dummy that could not speak. I finally managed to get the words out. "Yes that would be fantastic" I told him, and also thanked him for showing me the carcass. I arranged to meet either him or one of his colleagues at the practice to finalise the time. Later on that day I went the short distance up the road to the vet's practice. I spoke with the stable hand Nigel, who had heard the noises from the field. "At first I thought it was an Owl" he told me, "but when I shone the torch down the field the eyes I saw were definitely not an owl". He chuckled briefly. "Anycase, an owl doesn't run across a field on all fours". "You actually saw it" I remarked. "Yeah" he replied, "third time this year but don't tell the boss, though I'm sure he know about it, but knowing him he'll want to shoot it". "What colour was it?" I asked. "Same as last time. Black, and also big, with a long tail". He gestured towards the stables behind. "There's an old tent in there if you want to use it as cover, it may rain this and next week, best to be organised", he told me. I went up with Nigel on four or five occasions before I started to stake out the field. A friend, Guy, was a big help and brought up flasks and sandwiches for me on a couple of occasions. Over the next few weeks I sat out overlooking from the top of the field. I was well protected from behind and had a full scope of the field and the valley. In a word, nothing, not even the local rabbit population, made an appearance. I felt I should wander about, but I decided against it. Just my luck that I would walk across the top boundary and then miss out on something that might be around at the other end.

I seriously began to think that it was body odour, as I had stopped using any scented products in case they were picked up by anything. Paranoia set in again. To the West of the valley were the Gramercy school and grounds, and I had always promised myself that I was going to give the area a good scouting over. These times were growing nearer and nearer. The grounds were teeming with rabbits and pheasants, including a completely white female. I often wondered how she had survived so long; she stood out like a black bear in a snowstorm.

Just as it seemed that I was going to get down to some serious staking out, my partner at the time created mighty havoc and insisted that I thought more of the cats, and also that I gave them more attention. I stayed quiet and said all the right things in the right places...well, one has to be sensible at times. I did say that if she was that worried she could come and spend some nights out in the field with me, but she never did. Over the next few weeks I did spend more time her, but couldn't help feeling that I had missed not only the boat, but also the cat, so to speak.

When I finally did venture out again it was during daylight hours. I had wandered aimlessly until I got to the Kennels road which ran across the South West boundary of Higher Brixham. There was a fantastic view from many places along the road with plenty of possibilities for staking out, and along this road was the rear end to Gramercy Grounds. There were also many other places where animals of all sizes could gain entry to the grounds. I would have to wait a very long time before I could actually get into the grounds, eventually gaining access when it had closed down as a school. As always, as I walked I mapped the area, including the fields on the other side of the boundary road.

I found a Westerly facing sloping field in which I sat with my back to a low wall. From here I could scan over a fair distance of the landscape, and well into the Galmpton Parish. There were a myriad of fields, copses and orchards, all with what seemed an endless amount of wildlife. On this particular day I saw buzzards circling and sparrowhawks diving in and around the hedgerows; one moment there, the next disappearing with a shrill alarm call from the birds it was targeting. I made reams of notes and drew sketches which I thought might come in useful at a latter date. I was entranced and almost transfixed by all the sights and sounds, when out to the left of my vision I saw something moving up along the field close to its boundary line. I turned completely towards whatever it was, and saw an animal move into some bushes. I saw the tail end of an animal I ascertained to be black, and also a substantially sized tail trailing behind it that seemed to sweep down and then curve up like an antenna. By this time I was standing with my binoculars fixed to my eyes. The animal reappeared as it jumped up effortlessly onto the bank of the field and ran alongside the wall which bordered it. As a head turned and looked in my direction, I fought to hold the binoculars steady and attached to my eyes. It was definitely a cat, not huge, but certainly a lot bigger than a domestic. It gazed over its left shoulder towards me for what seemed like an age. Its eyes, golden and glaring, fixed towards me. Then, with what seemed like an infinite ease, it turned its head forward and jumped over the wall. With one, maybe two, purposefully graceful movements it had disappeared down on to the Galmpton footpath. It had disappeared as quickly at it had appeared.

I was thrilled and elated, but still I muttered utterances about not having a decent camera. My brain was trying to work out exactly what it was I had seen. The cat was big, not huge but between medium and large. I could not work out what species it was. Many years later, learning from others who had better insight than what I had at the time, I am now sure that the cat was a crossbreed or a hybrid; definitely not a domestic by the size, shape, and the way that the ears were very upright and pointed.

The weather had been excellent with good visibility. There were trees nearby but not enough to overhang or give any shade to obstruct the view of what I had seen. When I came to my senses I waited a while before moving towards the spot on the bank where it stood. I searched for prints, but the ground was firm and hard and gave away nothing at all. I wanted to follow after the cat, but I had to cautious and sensible as I was alone and no one knew exactly where I was. From that day on, I always told someone of my whereabouts. I gathered up all my possessions from near the wall, left the field and continued along the road towards Hillhead. From there I turned back down onto the road that leads into Brixham. Although I did not note much with pen and paper on the return trip, my mind and senses were still alert to all the tracks and lanes that were between the kennels road and the *Watermans Arms*. It was time for a well deserved drink.

I returned to the area three days later with Kevin, a friend, and we walked down onto the footpath that leads towards Galmpton. Where the path went deeper into the valley we came across a stream that criss-crossed and fed many fields and gullies. This cool, clear, refreshing water may well have quenched the thirst of a passing feline; big, small, whatever it may be. As we looked and listened for any clues I realised the enormity of the situation in relation to the size of the localised area. I turned to Kevin and remarked that we had to keep the area constantly monitored. More bodies were needed to scan and patrol the surrounding terrain. He nodded in agreement, and we both looked up at a buzzard up over-head. The valley was a cauldron of heat and a hive of wildlife activity. An Eden of prey to whatever predators might hunt and patrol the valley, as they may have done for longer than we have known.

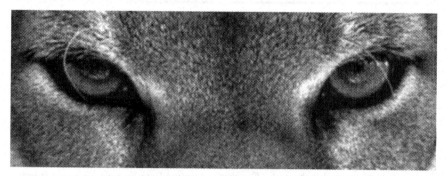

Northumbrian Big Cat Diaries
by Ian Bond

• *I have a lifelong interest in animals and in my mid-thirties I dropped back into education and managed to emerge with a degree in Environmental Biology. I now work as a Local Authority ecologist but like to think of myself as a naturalist first and foremost. A few years back, I managed to make the semi-final of BBC Radio 4's "Wildbrain" quiz two years running, but never quite managed to make the final. My main interests are bats, small mammals and herptiles. I particularly enjoy recording wildlife and last year managed to find two new harvest mouse records in County Durham, the first for 20 years, which was extremely satisfying. My ambitions are to learn French and to prove the existence of Bigfoot; I'm not sure which is the most difficult!*

Here in the North East sightings tend to occur in three main areas: the Tyne/ Derwent Valley corridor, the extensive conifer plantations that fringe the Cleveland Hills and the area of South Durham that very approximately corresponds with Tony Blair's constituency boundary. Despite having lots of 'wild' upland areas where a puma might feel at home, we are not exactly a hot spot for big cat sightings, with only a few reports coming to light each year. Continuing this pattern, the few sightings that have been reported to me this year have all come from these three areas.

The year started off with a pretty definite record when a farmer near Consett claimed to have seen a big cat chase a deer over a fence into a small wood and then kill it. Not much chance of mistaken identity with that one. A roe deer carcass was later found which had the hair licked off parts of its body. Unfortunately, the article in the *Evening Gazette* didn't describe the cat. I think this is because the press and public seem to assume that if it's a big cat it must be black, though this doesn't help those of us who are trying to work out possible distribution patterns for the various species.

Another encounter in this area was in early July when a large, "panther" type cat was seen by a family near Tynedale. What was possibly the same animal was seen shortly afterwards at Duke's Wood, Hexham, when what was described as a large cat walked across the path in front of a dog walker. The encounters were recorded in the Hexham Courant, but unfortunately it doesn't seem to have bothered with details such as colour, how big "large" constitutes, or how soon after "shortly afterwards" was.

Moving to the most southerly of our big cat 'hot spots' (I should really call them 'luke warm' spots), a large black cat was seen at Pinchinthorpe, near Guisborough. This was in early August when, around 1am, the cat leapt across the road in front of a car. The driver and passenger estimated that it was 3' high with a body about 4' long plus the tail. The driver's immediate thought was that it was an Afghan Hound, by which I take it she meant big with a long tail, rather than resembling an emaciated, four-legged womble. She also reckoned that had they been going any faster they would have hit it, which would have definitely put Pinchinthorpe on the map.

Most of the records that I get are from around Tony's patch, perhaps not surprisingly as that's where I work and the first two records are not that far from where I live.

One was by a water board inspector who saw a big, black cat from a distance of about 50m. The cat walked in front of two stacks of bricks, which the inspector later measured as being 40'' apart. The cat's body, minus the tail, was the length of the gap. I'm not sure of the exact location that my informant was trying to describe, but it was definitely in the Eaglescliffe, Urlay Nook area, and would have only been a couple of miles from Burn Wood; where it had previously been reported that a deer carcase had been found up a tree. The other record was from Middleton St George, which is just a couple of miles from Burn Wood in the other direction. A friend of my informant had seen a big, black cat there on two occasions at the beginning of the year. Finally, the Trimdon Panther put in another appearance in mid October when a local farmer saw it cross the road, lit up by his headlights, whilst he was unfastening a gate.

All in all another typically quiet year up here in the North East, though with at least a couple of tantalising sightings that would be hard to write off as anything other than a big cat. In spite of this paucity of sightings the records all add to the general picture and, to my mind, a pattern does seem to be emerging. Anyway, if the big cats were too obvious it wouldn't be anywhere near as fascinating.

DNA
by Chris Johnston

● *Chris Johnston is a Liverpool based researcher with many years experience. He also takes a special interest in the events down in sunny Devon, and makes several trips there every year.*

DNA testing is now widely used in many areas of scientific research. Testing is an option for any big cat investigator, and could be used as conclusive evidence of a big cat in the British Isles. In 2005, for the first time, I used the services of a testing centre to identify a species. To have the test completed can be expensive, and it is something that I would not do very often. In this case the faeces tested were taken from a back garden in a remote area of the Lake District.

In 2003 a lady was awoken in the night by the sound of her front gates rattling. She quickly jumped out of bed to see if there was an intruder about; looking out of her bedroom window she saw a big black cat looking up at her. There are two large plant containers in the garden, standing 18 inches high, and the cat towered above them. The lady and the cat looked at one another for a while, then the cat walked off around the side of the house. From this time onwards, large cat like paw prints have been found regularly along with scrapings (a cat uses its back legs to make a mound from the earth). The most consistent and interesting behaviour is that every few weeks from October to March the cat deposits droppings on top of a large plant in the garden.

In December 2004 droppings were left again, and this time we decided to have them DNA tested. It was the only sure way of knowing what type of cat it was. If faeces are going to be tested they have to be collected straight away and placed in the freezer; it is also important that no cross contamination occurs, so it is best to wear gloves. DNA is extracted from the outside of the faeces, so if they are left in the sunlight the DNA can be damaged. With it being the Christmas period we decided to leave them in the freezer until the New Year. After Christmas they were sent for testing and two weeks after we received the results.

Droppings found in the Lake District: Pictures courtesy of Chris Johnston.

Sadly, the results were not what we wanted but were however very interesting. They were not from a big cat, but no exact match could be found on their data base. The conclusion was that the most likely candidate was a Scottish Wildcat. The faeces that we had tested looked so much as if they were from a big cat, and the way in which they were left was consistent with typical big cat behaviour.

We have now placed a remote camera in the garden overlooking the plant where the droppings have been left; hopefully by means of a photograph we may be able to identify the animal that visits the garden.

Faeces from a Leopard
by Mark Fraser

"In the Darkness on the Edge of Town..."
(Bruce Springsteen 1978)

● *Since I was a small boy I have had a great interest in sightings of animals that just should not be there. Over the years that interest has grown, and it is not just confined to the big cats but includes all manner of weird and wonderful creatures that are reported throughout Britain. I have been investigating sightings for the last 15 years in Scotland and Yorkshire but it wasn't until November 2003 that I saw my first big cat.*

I am not a big cat expert, but as I have spent the last 15 years investigating sightings in this country I am quite knowledgeable on the history of the big cat saga in the UK. The evidence I gather, and have gathered in the past is presented to the real big cat experts, and those people in various fields whose knowledge is needed at certain times. Also, after 15 years you do learn a thing or two.

As a researcher I am always asking people to report their experiences to me. So to be fair I shall relate here my own sightings of big cat-like animals. In the past I have seen glimpses of animals in the distance that could, maybe, have been mystery big cats, but nothing definite that could have made me say for sure. Most vigils are like this.

The first time I saw an animal that left me wondering was in the Glenshee Mountains of Scotland, around August 1994 (a very strange year for me and my family). This area is a beautiful place where the fairies play even today. Unfortunately on this occasion it was dark, around midnight, and we could not see anything apart from the odd herd of deer running along the roadside lit up in our headlights, and the countless German camper vans parked in lay-bys.

I do not recall the exact spot, but we were heading South on the A93 and going uphill, when from our left, a largish animal ran right across our path. It seemed

---

to turn its head to look at us whilst running, then it disappeared into the blackness on our right. It gave me a strange and eerie feeling as the car headlights reflected the eyes a bright red; in fact, they were almost glowing. It was roughly the size of a fully grown Labrador, to pinch a phrase.

It first put me in mind of a cross between a kangaroo and a hyena. Don't ask me why, it's just what flitted through my mind at the time! When I read the next issue of *Animals & Men* (issue 6), I even likened it to the nandi bear! But in reality I simply do not know what it was; other than that it could have been a cat, and it certainly wasn't a deer.

Several hours later, as we reached a fairly built up area on the outskirts of Glasgow, I remarked to my wife what a funny looking dog it was sat in the lay by on the side of the road. She replied with something like "are you sure it was a dog?". With that we were gone and unable to turn around. Only three weeks before this night I had seen my first wolf in Scotland, on the outskirts of the small village of Drummuir. I had also heard its howls ... but that is another story.

Over the years, especially on vigils, we see large cat-like animals just on the edge of our vision during the night. Or during the daylight, again just that little too far away. As if they know that if they come just a few feet closer we will identify them and the game will be up. One unknown animal played hide and seek with myself and Brian Murphy while we were on a vigil in rainy Lincolnshire. It kept on darting in and out of a bush, running a few feet then running back in. It was rather strange. I had the small binoculars with me, and by the time I had returned from the car with the larger ones the animal had had enough of its game and came out of the bush no more. Incidentally, there was a sighting made in that area that night, although unfortunately not by us.

The first time I saw an animal that I could say without a shadow of a doubt was definitely a mystery cat was, again, in Lincolnshire. It was the 19th of November 2003, and we were on a vigil based at Julie and Sandy Richardson's home. You may remember Sandy, as he became famous with the Hemingby 'cat in the caravan', and was the first to have hairs analysed with results claiming that they most definitely came from a leopard.

Anyway, myself, Chris Mullins, Brian Murphy and Terry Dye, who had just joined us that evening about an hour earlier, were sat in Sandy and Julie's front room watching the Scotland game. At 22.10hrs the phone rang, and Julie answered it. On the other end was a very excited woman who claimed she had just seen a very large black cat on the outskirts of Horncastle at around 22.00hrs. She described it as the size of a fully grown Labrador with a long sweeping 'S' shaped tail, not far from the sewage works. The four of us decided to go and have a look for ourselves straight away. I got in the passenger seat with Terry Dye, and Chris drove his car with Brian. We maintained communication between the two cars via walkie-talkie radios.

After a couple of wrong turnings we finally managed to find the right road, and the sewage works. Having passed the works we turned in a lane. As Terry negotiated his three-point turn the headlights hit a very large black cat running across the field towards trees against the sewage work's fence. I shouted for Brian and Chris who were in the car behind, and who for some reason shot on up the road towards the sewage work's gates.

The cat was about as large as a fully grown Alsatian, I personally didn't see the tail. I agreed with Terry when he described it as "black, almost fluffy", and with a long coat. No other details were seen, although I think the distance we were away from the cat was a fair bit further then 20ft, as someone later said. My estimation was maybe three times that distance.

I wasted no time and actually jumped out of Terry's car and into the field after this big black cat. I wanted to know what it was and after 15 years of investigating other people's sightings, this was my chance. I ran down the side of the trees and bushes where the cat was last seen heading. I stopped half way down the field thinking that the animal must have gone away out of view by now. I turned round and the torch beam caught two dull green/yellowy eyes, belonging to the cat that was sat on it haunches looking at me. I half thought it was an amused look, but quickly brushed that aside. It was about 15 -20ft away, obscured by foliage as the eyes peered out at me.

At that point Brian came on the radio, asking what was happening. I calmly told him that the cat was sat watching me, a spitting distance away. I don't think he realised quite what I was saying, but after a few expletives he got the message. From this distance, the cat appeared to be about 2 and a half feet high and seemed to have lost its rough look, instead appearing sleek, calm and knowing! I slowly (some would say foolishly, but I knew this was no leopard) walked outwards in an arc, straying a little further out into the field so I would not come too close. But on my walk down I must have passed it at a distance of 2ft when it stopped to watch me. The cat must have ducked down and slinked away under the fence into the sewage works, because it was there and then the next instant it wasn't. My attention was distracted by the noise of the walkie talkie, and it could have made its escape in one of those moments.

I had lost it, and I returned to the cars and my three comrades in arms, who had never once ventured of the roadside! I scoured the area for another 15 minutes, and then returned to the scene of the sighting. Again on my own, I went into the field to look for any tracks the cat may have left behind, but in the darkness I found nothing. We returned to Hemingby and the hospitality of Sandy & Julie.

The next day, having returned home, we learnt that video footage had been taken a couple of hours earlier in the same area outside of Horncastle. I know nothing of the footage or what it shows. This cat certainly was busy that evening, showing itself at least three times that we know of. But as Chris Mullins

Brian Murphy stood in the spot where the cat watched me.

pointed out, it was bin night; no wheelie bins in the area, just black bags. Hundreds of them lined along the roads and streets. What exactly it was that I saw, I do not know. I know that it wasn't a leopard or a puma, but I do believe that the cat I saw was the one locals dub the 'panther of the Wolds' or the 'Lindsey leopard'."

It was six months later, on the 16th of July 2004, when I was to have my next sighting. I was sitting in my car just off Glassford Road in Strathaven, Scotland. I was actually at work, and part of my work at the time occasionally involved sitting and watching. It was dusk and the street light had just come on, giving off an orange glow. The last thing on my mind was big cats.

As I sat there I saw a largish brown animal walk down the track and stop on the left of the track opposite, which leads into woods. I actually could not make out what it was at first; due to an incident at work the previous week my left eye was completely shut and the right still a touch blurry. This animal then walked into the undergrowth on the left and I never gave it another thought.

Five minutes later I idly watched a fox walk down the road and onto the grass verge. When it reached the tree trunk on the right of me it stopped dead. Every muscle in its body went taught and it looked ready to run, but it didn't. At that point I looked up and saw the animal I had seen earlier; it was also stood stock still and watching the fox.

By that point I could see that what I was looking at was a cat, although it was also on the edge of the orange glow that the street light gave off. It stood twice the height, maybe a touch more, of the fox, and maybe a length longer. It had a domestic cat's face with short, pointed ears. On its chest was a large white patch in its tawny coloured coat. These two animals must have stood and stared at each other for over a minute, not one of them moving until a car came by in the lane. The fox shot off up the grass verge to the right and the large cat ran up the small track out of view.

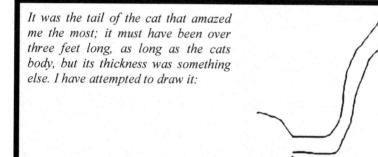

It was the tail of the cat that amazed me the most; it must have been over three feet long, as long as the cats body, but its thickness was something else. I have attempted to draw it:

I didn't look for tracks on the ground straight away, as I wanted the animal to come back. It did not; in fact, I was in that spot for the next three days but never saw the cat again. The next morning I did not find any tracks, but on the next evening I did find several cat-like impressions which I tried to protect so I could make casts. Alas, when I returned several days later they had been obliterated. I also had no camera in the car, ironic as my wife Hannah had bought me a brand new one that very day for my birthday. I had taken it out of the car, along with night vision goggles, that morning as I thought I would not need them at work.

About 20 minutes after the cat had left I suddenly looked out of my car window to the right, and there not more then twenty feet away was a small ginger Tom sat on the grass watching me. I winked at it, the cat blinked back then stood up and walked away!

My third and final sighting to date came in September of this year on another vigil, this time on the outskirts of Monaghan Town in the Irish Republic. It was obviously not technically a sighting of a British big cat, but a big cat in a country where they are not supposed to exist nonetheless.

Stills from the footage taken by Charlie McGuinness,

We had gone over at the request of a local businessman, Charlie Mcguinness. He had actually visited me in Scotland a couple of months previously, bringing along video footage of a mysterious black cat that he had made in fields behind his house during July 2004. The local media swooped and for some unknown, unfathomable reason, instead of printing a still from Mr McGuinness's footage they took a picture of a local cat with a white blaze on its chest and printed that instead. Even stranger, was that the cat belonged to the paper's editor.

After suffering ridicule due mainly to this picture, Charlie is on somewhat of a mission to prove that a big black cat, dubbed the 'Beast of Monaghan' or the 'Beast of the Border' actually exists.

As we sometimes find on vigils, depending on who we visit and who comes along, they can be rather like a holiday. This was proving to be one of those instances. We were treated the whole time with great hospitality, much Guinness and good food. One drawback though was that we hardly slept; there just wasn't the time.

Anyway, after several days of meeting witnesses and scouring woods and fields we finally came to the last night. Those present were myself, Charlie, Sandy Smith and our new friend John Nutley, originally from Dublin. Charlie wanted us to check out an area that previous black cat reports had come from. It was getting dark, so after parking up on the roadside we each got out a torch. Being the last night, they were nearly all out of charge. We never took any other equipment with us (i.e. night vision), as we thought we were just going to have a bit of a recce.

Halfway through the forest we heard horses running and birds taking flight ahead. After successfully negotiating several electric and barbed wire fences, a steep hillock and a boggy forest, we emerged in a clearing below. We entered a field, whereupon Charlie began to tell us of a sighting which occurred in the exact spot where we were stood. Basically, a farmer out in his tractor had been startled by a large black cat running out of the field to his right, running across his path and disappearing into the forest in more or less the same spot that we emerged from. This occurred in July 2004. Also a dead, partially eaten rabbit was found, which may have been eaten by the cat. At that point we heard a rumbling, pounding sound. I thought it could be a train, but when my torch lit up about 20 pairs of eyes racing towards us, it took me a little time to realise that the noise was horse's hooves, and that the eyes belonged to a herd that was coming our way at a very great speed. Someone shouted "lets get out of here", and we all turned to run. But Charlie said stop, and when the horses arrived they stopped with inches to spare and he calmed them. Phew! The rest of our hearts were pounding louder then the horses' hooves, as we genuinely thought we were going to be trampled.

We carried on walking along the edge of the field, with the forest to our left.

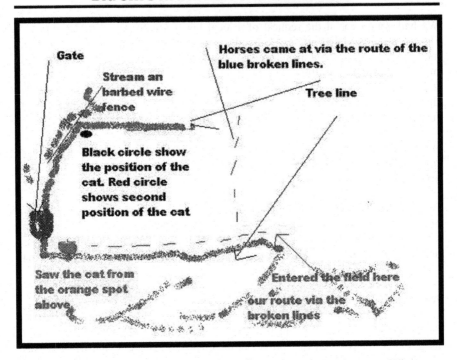

Across the field was another row of trees, about 200 - 300 yards away. When we first came into the forest Charlie was a little ahead of us, and he now told us that in front of him he kept hearing twigs snapping on the forest floor. He could not see what was doing it, only hear that they seemed to be the same distance away, moving ahead of us. I began to wonder what had made the horses stampede, and what was breaking the twigs, as whatever it was would have got into the clearing before us.

We reached the far corner of the field (marked on the map below), and Charlie asked "what's that?". We looked, and all saw a pair of greeny/yellow eyes that lit up in our torch beam. As our eyes adjusted, we saw that these eyes belonged to a sleek, jet-black body that was at least three feet long. It slowly dawned on us we were looking at the Monaghan mystery cat, or one of them, and that it was watching us just as intently. With the light we could only just make it out, but we were certain of what we were seeing. It moved another two or three times, but only a few feet. It then moved slowly to the left and stood sideways on, with its head turned towards us.

We stood there for about four to five minutes, then I suggested that we walk slowly across the field as our torch-lights were fading fast and we would soon be seeing nothing. The stand off was getting us nowhere. After we'd taken about ten steps, the cat turned and swiftly shot into the undergrowth behind it.

When we reached the spot where the cat had stood there was a small stream, and behind that a barbed wire fence and trees. I looked and never saw it, but John and Sandy did; the cat had not moved far at all but was stood about 50 feet away. It soon ran off again, but what they did see left them in no doubt that the animal was a leopard.

At that, a motorbike roared in the distance. We all momentarily thought it was the roar of a cat, then chuckled. It was at that point I noticed that the horses had stopped following us, and where standing in the middle of the field. It was only when we reached them that they resumed walking behind us and followed us all the way to the gate, which had an electric wire running along it which we only just noticed in time.

It was decided to come back the next day in daylight to check for tracks or any 0000signs that the cat may have left behind. Unfortunately, myself and Sandy were to catch the ferry back early the next morning, so the job was left to Charlie and John. We headed back to the cars, across the fields and even more electric fences, barbed wire and various other unspeakable things you stand in when it's dark. One or two members of the party were still a little apprehensive, not wanting to spend any more time in the dark.

What we did see was a cat, I am sure of that. But I wonder, did it actually walk ahead of us in the forest, making the horses stampede in the clearing and crossing the field before us? It was just as interested in us as we were in it, but knew of our presence long before we were aware of it. It obviously showed no aggression, and while not rushing to leave the area, it always kept its distance from us.

Mark Fraser

MYSTERY
CAT DIARY
2005
COMPILED BY
MARK FRASER

JANUARY

1st: Ayrshire/Scotland. Lampers spotted a large, 3ft high black cat, on the A78 Irvine by-pass close by to the Paper Mill. The animal simply stopped to look at the witnesses before it carried on its way. The lampers did not attempt to shoot the cat, and reported that they have never seen anything like it before. *(source: Mark Fraser)*.

2nd: Devon/England. A sketchy report of something black and cat-like around Holne and Poundsgate. Vennford Reservoir has also had many sightings over the years, and prints and droppings have been found here. *(source: Alan White)*.

3rd: MOD/England. A deer was found dead by the side of the road during daylight hours. 15 minutes later, when the driver returned along the route, he was quite surprised that the carcass had gone. No other people were in the area. Whatever moved it was strong enough to take away a fully grown roe deer, in a very short space of time. *(source:Mark Fraser: undisclosed location)*.

4th: Cambridgeshire/England. Andy Williams was contacted by David Fuller from the Cambridgeshire Paranormal Research Society with the following:

"I am a member of Cambridge Paranormal research Society. We have for the last two years been monitoring possible sightings of Big Cats in Cambridge-shire, and have recently been in contact with people around Oakington near Cambridge. We had a phone call from one of these people today (04/01/05) who said they had the remains of a dead lamb from their farm. I will be collecting the remains of this animal tomorrow, which I will be photographing. The farm owner informs us that only the head and backbone are left of the animal, and there is only a small amount of skin still on it. I am under the impression that the lamb has only recently gone missing. Also near the remains, there was animal dropping with lamb fur in it. The remains were moved from the location by the farmer over the Christmas/New Year period, to preserve what was left. I presume they did not take the droppings.

All this could be nothing out of the ordinary, depending how long the animal had been missing/killed. There may be foxes or other animals around the fields that might strip a carcass like this, I have no idea. My thoughts are that the carcass may be of some importance, again depending on the state of it, and whether your group would want someone to examine it, as this sort of thing is not our speciality." *(source: Andy Williams).*

4th: Aberdeenshire/Scotland. A large black cat seen at the end of a driveway to a croft near Insch. This was the scene of a horse attack on the 18th of December 2004. Green eyes, scruffy looking, as big as a large Labrador dog, jet-black ears set low, broad chested, sat in bushes. *(source: Mark Fraser).*

4th: Renfrewshire (Kilmacolm)/Scotland. An elderly lady witnessed what she claimed was a huge black cat coming out of the ground and running past her. She became very frightened after this experience, and her little dog "has not been right since".

The area was in fact an old railway bridge, and there is indeed a way that an animal can enter and appear out of the hole at the other end. On witnessing this, it would at first seem that the cat had emerged from the ground. *(source: Greenock Telegraph)*

5th: Gloucestershire/England. Large prints found in a back garden of a house in Dymock, believed by the witness to belong to a big cat. *(source: Mark Fraser).*

5th: Devon/England. Recieved a telephone call this morning from a chap in Totnes. He was out walking his dog yesterday afternoon (5/1/05) between 4-5pm on the south side of the River Dart, down towards the sluice gate brook area. He saw a movement across the river which he first took to be a dog, but which on closer inspection turned out to be a large brown coloured cat. It seemed to be patrolling or scouting around the edge of the second banked field along the river walkway towards Asprington. The man said he thought that the cat may have caught something, because it moved suddenly and sharply to one side and then seemed to have something in it's mouth. It then turned and walked off towards a small plantation copse, where the man lost sight of it.

On returning home, he checked in some books and told me that he thought it may have been a Puma/Cougar. On checking with him he informed me that the visibility was good, and that he was certain of what he had seen, with the Cat being 4 to 6 feet in total length and a mid to darker brown colour. He also knew that in the past that there had been cat sightings around the areas both sides of the river, but seemed totally at ease with the encounter.

Kevin is going over today to have a word with him

As for the Totnes sighting, both Keith and Kevin went to have a look around the area, and about four fields from where the original sighting took place they must have disturbed it. The animal took a brief look at them and then tore away at a rate of knots. Keith got his camera phone up and clicked, but it was so far in the distance by then it was indistinguishable in the photo. Both said that it was definitely a puma by the movement, gait and the tail. *(source: Alan White).*

Circa 5th: Hampshire/England. (source: Nigel Spencer & Colin Lacey). I was working at Soberton Heath this week and the dairy had an "intruder". It left 4 inch prints in the soft clay and scared one of their workers. Described as like a panther, black and very big. The dairy is Watsons, Hawks Nest Farm, Bere road, Soberton Heath, Fareham, Hants

On the 30th Colin Lacey reports:

Yesterday afternoon myself, Jen Gillibrand and family visited the area around Hawks Nest dairy farm where Nigel had reported a sighting of a big black cat. Findings were as follows:

Golf course - staff have seen prints left in the sand in bunkers, and one sighting of a large black cat has been reported within the last year. Photos were taken of prints, but the man we spoke to was not sure if they were still around.

House at farm entrance - Mr Dewey who lives here has large-ish black dogs, although these appear to be elderly and are not allowed to roam free. He has not seen anything and had not heard of the other sightings.

Farm - The only worker we found hadn't seen anything or heard of anyone seeing anything. He suggests it may have been a visiting engineer that saw it.

Next house down, beyond the dairy - has a sandy coloured whippet type dog, not big or black, which is disturbed at the same approximate time every night, barks etc. and defends her territory. Had it been a fox, she would have chased it, not stood her ground. This has been happening for 3 weeks, which ties in with Nigel's report.

General terrain - dense woodland surrounded by farmland and golf course. Even with no leaves on the trees, it is difficult to see far into it at all. Plenty of food - rabbits, sheep, deer. Nearby river and disused railway.

6th: Devon/England. Sighting of a large black cat on the north side of Chagford, spotted in half light. *(source: Alan White).*

8th: Renfrewshire/Scotland. Mrs F was in her house (Kilmacolm) during the evening when she heard a loud roaring noise coming from her garden. She describes this as being very scary as she was in the house herself.

Curiosity got the better of her, and she went out to see where all the noise was coming from. As she opened her door, a large black cat which she describes as being a "leopard-like creature" ran out in front of her and over the wall into her neighbour's garden.

A couple of days later, on the 11th, her daughter June was taking the dogs out for the night when she noticed a large black cat crossing the garden and going over the wall into Bridge of Weir Road and a neighbour's garden. *(source: Greenock Telegraph).*

Date unknown: Essex/England. A large black animal believed by some to be a big cat spotted crossing fields near Ongar. Later large prints were found. *(source: unknown).*

9th: Enfield/England. Hello, today whilst out flying a kite with my children in Trent Park, Hadley Road end, Enfield, I spotted a big black cat in the woods. It caught my eye as it ran through the woods, at first I thought it was a dog but the way it moved caught my attention. It had a long black tail and the only thing I could compare it to is a black panther. I had not heard about any other sightings of these creatures but when I told my father he told me other people had seen big cats in Trent Park before. The animal did not look scared and did not look like it was stalking anything but seemed to be just running through the woods. Being a big animal lover and having owned both cats and dogs before I am very aware of the way both animals move. I am therefore convinced that was a big cat that I saw, the trouble is my family, who were there at the time think I'm completely mad! *(source: BCIB report form).*

10th January 2005: Renfrewshire/Scotland. A bus driver claims he spotted a large black cat near Kilmacolm Cross. *(source: Greenock Telegraph)*

10th: Shropshire/England. A female witness who does not wish to be named, reported a seeing a large black cat while driving home from work at around 20.00hrs. She reported that the cat was running up the embankment towards Telford town centre as she drove down the slip road to get on at junction five of the M54 in the Shrewsbury direction. She describes the animal as being "very fast, as big as a Dalmation dog with smooth black hair." *(source: Shropshire Star)*

11th: Renfrewshire/Scotland. A large black cat seen along the Bridge of Weir road in Kilmacolm. *(source: Greenock Telegraph).*

11th: Renfrewshire/Scotland. Mrs. Mc was out walking her dog on the cycle track making for the Bridge of Weir. She walks on the track regularly and on this occasion as she approached North Denniston there was a woman with a dog walking towards her in the Kilmacolm direction. The two of them witnessed what Mrs Mc describes as being a large black cat which she believes to be a leopard-like creature. She went on to say that it walked underneath the railway bridge at North Denniston heading in the direction of the Duchal Wood at Pinewood Fishery. *(source: Greenock Telegraph).*

11th: Argyllshire/Scotland. "I was with my ex-father law today on a business trip. As we were chatting in the car, coming up to the village of Clachan, he mentioned that he'd seen a large black cat cross the road there a few weeks ago. You can imagine, that I nearly jumped out of my skin. He had no idea that I was interested in this or my involvement with the British Big Cat Group. I thought my ex-wife had mentioned it to him, but obviously not.

"To give you some background, my ex-father in law drives to Glasgow from Campbeltown, (130miles distance), every Tuesday, (for the past 30 odd years) to pick up stock for his Wines and Spirits wholesale business. Leaving Campbeltown about 5am and arriving in Glasgow at 8am.

"On Tuesday 11th January, at 5:30am, driving along the A83, through Clachan village. (You have to slow at this point because of a blind right turn in the road). A large black cat ran across the road from left to right, no more than 5 or 6 metres in front of the van. Lit from the headlights and the streetlights, it ran from the bushes crossed the road past the village garage. He described it as a very large black cat, which ran with its tail out straight in line with its body. Estimating the size is relatively easy as he said the tail was the length of the small path as it crossed the road. Checking dimensions at the site, he said that the body was about 4 foot and the tail about 2 foot. He didn't see any eyes as it just ran out without looking.

"When we returned back to Campbeltown today, I showed him a few pictures of various melanistic cats without telling him the actual average sizes of each species. He picked out a picture of a Black Leopard, saying that the head and especially the tail was exactly what he saw.

"On checking a leopard's dimensions, I found that on average their body length is 48" and tail of 24". Exactly the estimate of size of the cat he saw.

I'm extremely jealous of his sighting, but considering he's one of a few people who travel this route regularly and this early, if anyone was going to see anything, he was. Although its the first time he's seen anything in decades of driving. Curiously, as we were driving back today, approaching the clachan area, we were chatting about the sighting, when we saw a large black animal in a field to our left, near a farmhouse. It was about 200 metres away. Slightly larger than a sheep, (we could tell by the sheep in the next field), about the size of a large Alsation, or Collie. It appeared to be sniffing the ground.

"We both thought "No, couldn't be". However it disappeared as we drove past.

I couldn't really tell if it was Dog or Big Cat, however my gut feeling at the time, was that it was a dog, (although there was no owner in sight). Still I'm never going to be sure 100% though

"An interesting day after all." *(source: Shaun Stephens).*

14th: Devon/England. Have had a phone call from Ipplepen way this morning, Tony is going out to have a scout around. This sighting was of a brownish animal around some farm out-buildings, and very close to a garden-come-animal centre. *(source: Alan White).*

15th: Yorkshire/England. A large black cat spotted in fields outside Buroughbridge, near Steve Newlove's farm. A local lady saw a large animal in the road standing over a road kill rabbit. As she approached it ran into a field. This was near Aldwark bridge. *(source: Mark Fraser).*

15th : Moray/Scotland. Large black cat spotted at 16.15 hours at Glenferness on Saturday, approx twice the size of domestic cat. *(source: BCIB report form).*

16th: Leicestershire/England. We have received a report from one of my father's relatives that their domestic cat has been found killed and buried in their garden at Glen Parva, South Leicester. There was a lot of blood where it was killed and also a very strong smell of ammonia near the greenhouse. Other than that, there is no other link, apart from sightings in that area. *(source: Nigel Spencer).*

17th - Lanarkshire/Scotland. "I would like to report a sighting of a cat-like animal I saw whilst walking my dog last night. At first I saw three deer in a local park where I walk my dog. The dog startled the deer which ran away, naturally the dog attempted to pursue them but they disappeared. I stood for a moment to see if I could see them, I looked along a path which has no obstructions and noticed a dark figure lying on the ground about 50 yards away, I thought it may have been one of the deer but as I started to walk towards it, it calmly got up and walked into nearby trees, it was only when it got up I realised it wasn't a deer as it had a tail almost the length of its body, I would guess it was twice the size of my dog which is a two-year old Labrador. I live in the north of Glasgow in a built up area and was wondering if any sightings of an animal of this type have been reported before in this area.

"My sighting took place in Robroyston park, I went into the park at an entrance on Rockfield Road, Barmulloch, G21. The entrance is a gravel path (30 yards approx.) with a kid's school on the left, my sighting was at the rear of the school, which borders the park. The school's name is Gadburn Primary, a special needs school, main entrance Rockfield Road. We more or less border the countryside here, with only a few private housing estates dotted around, before miles of fields. There is a railway track a few miles away close to the M80 Stepps by-pass. It has been over a week now, but whenever I close my eyes I immediately see a long dark tail." *(source: BCIB report form).*

21st: Boroughbridge, Yorkshire/England. "Thought you might be interested in my sighting this morning at 07.55 at Staveley near Boroughbridge, North Yorkshire.

It ran across the road in front of me and then across a field to my right. At first I thought it was a large dark fox but it was much bigger than any fox I have ever seen. The nearest thing I could liken it to is a black German Shepard, with a distinctive tail. I immediately telephoned my wife who told me that for the last three days our two dogs have "gone 'absolutely wild' having picked up the scent of something in a lane about 200m from where I spotted the creature." " *(source: BCIB report form).*

Exact date unknown: Oxfordshire/England. Stephen Thompson, of Ickleton Road, was pulling into his driveway at about 6pm in when he saw an animal about 10 yards in front of him.

The animal, which looked like a big black cat, then jumped over a four-foot fence.

Mr. Thompson, who runs a leisure and sports club in Newbury, said the animal was definitely not a deer or a dog, and the way it jumped was like a cat.

"It looked like a panther to me," he said. "It gave me a shock. I have never seen anything like it." *(source: Oxford Mail).*

Exact date unknown: Oxfordshire/England. The BBC News reports that an antelope at the Cotswold Wildlife Park was killed and partially eaten, the keepers, it reports, are convinced it had been killed by a large wildcat. *(source: BBC News).*

28th: Sutherland/Scotland. "I live in Embo, Dornoch, in Sutherland. I was working at a house today and noticed in a field opposite a sheet fleece hanging from some barbed wire. I also noticed a small piece of sheep laid in the field nearby.

"I asked the customer to have a look and he saw what I saw.

"I walked across the field and I found that what I thought was small piece of sheep was in fact the sheep. It's head was intact as was it's backbone and the back end. The ribs had been eaten down to stumps and all traces of flesh had gone. There was no trace of any guts or internal organs, but around the area there where spots of blood.

The Fleece in the barbed wire had been ripped off the body as it still had skin attached as well as blood. I have taken some photo's as proof in case the farmer removed it or it came back for the rest.

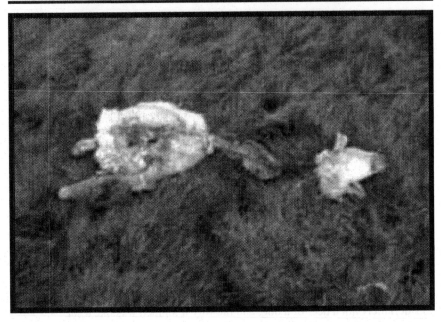

Sheep carcass found in Embo, Dornoch, in Sutherland.

Not a big cat, but a Scottish wildcat, caught in a cage in Aberdeenshire

"The sheep was not in the field last night as I left but it was there this morning."

(source: BCIB report form/pictures copyright of Chris Cogan).

28th: Somerset/England. "I live in Freshford near Bath, and this morning about 9.30am I discovered feathers from one my chickens. The other one has completely disappeared and no feathers have been found from it. I looked around the garden and discovered large prints in the soil, near the feathers. The prints are cat shaped and roughly 4-5 inches in diameter. There is also unturned soil around the area, and large scratch marks, the claws of the animals are long and have left deep holes in the soil. There is a possibility that they are from a wild cat as there have been sightings in our area before. About one year ago, somebody living in our house walked up the footpath in the night, and saw a large black animal escaping into the bushes. Because it was dark there is no guarantee it was anything significant but soon after that we lost 2 of our chickens. They were replaced and today we have lost both of them. There is a chance one of them is hiding somewhere (the one whose feathers we didn't find) but it seems the large cockarel has been eaten. "Obviously we don't know for certain whether this is a wild cat that has done this but if you know of anyone local to our area or who is willing to travel to identify the prints we will be very grateful. We have young children, and two pheasants so until we know for certain what this animal is we are concerned for their safety. Many of our neighbours have chickens, rabbits and cats too so it is important we find out whether they will be in danger." *(source: BCIB report form).*

28th January 2005: Aberdeenshire - Insch/Scotland. To protect livestock, crofters erected a steel cage in order to try and catch the large mysterious black cat. After an excited telephone call to Mark Fraser telling him that they had caught a big cat, who in return telephoned Sandy Smith to come and pick him up to hot foot it up to Abderdeenshire, as his car was not working; The pictures came through. Not a big cat, but a Scottish wildcat.

After four PWLOs from the district came to see the cat, as they had never seen a Scottish wildcat before, the animal was released, but only to be caught and then released again several days later. *(source:Mark Fraser).*

On-going, all years: Isle of Wight/England. Farmer A. (anonymous) has suffered a lot of livestock losses over the years and has had several sightings of a large sandy-coloured cat on his farm.

The cat has red eyes when seen in the dark, sheep are terrified of this animal and they have been seen stampeding the perimeter fences when it enters the field. They are also aware of its presence.

A farmer in a land rover spotted the cat while out waiting for it, chased it down a dead-end whereupon it scaled an MOD 7ft security fence with ease and escaped.

It has also been shot with a 2.2 and apparently wounded in early 2005, and again escaped.

Holidaymakers saw a large brown cat on the farm in the summer of 2003 and thought that the farmer actually kept cats on the land!

Sheep kills have been happening on this farm for at least five years *(source: Mark Fraser).*

Exact date unknown: Kent/England. A motorist saw a large black creature emerging from a wood in Coxheath Road, West Farleigh. Cat-like. *(source: This is Kent).*

Late January: Lincolnshire/England. Several sightings of a large black cat around the villages of Woodhall Spa, Kirkby on Bain and Ostlers Plantation. *(source:Sandy & Julie Richardson).*

21st January 2005: Yorkshire/England Thorpe Underwood, North Yorkshire. January Vigil by BCIB.

Chris Johnstone was the first to arrive in the afternoon, shortly followed by James Martin, the BBC camera man. I really couldn't be bothered with this vigil, my heart just wasn't in it, and after knocking off my wing mirror five minutes into the journey, I would have turned back if the other lads had not been there.

I had brought the wrong tent poles and could not find my head-torch; this was going pear-shaped from the beginning for me.

When I arrived, Ade, a likable lad from York was already there, setting up his tent. Steve Archibald and Chris J had already camped and James Martin (BBC Wildlife Unit) was filming the events. Andy Williams then arrived, this was the first time we had met at long last. Shortly after Chris Mullins from Beastwatch UK arrived and we were complete.

Myself and Andy set up the hide. James conducted more interviews and the rest of the lads went off into Bouroughbridge for food.

The first shift was Andy and Chris in the hide from 12 - 02.00rs. It was a bitterly cold night at -3. I retired to my tent and snuggled in. Chris Mullins then reported he saw a pair of eyes looking at us from about 100 yards away, but believed them to be too close to the ground to be a large cat. I called the lads in the hide on the walkie talkie, asking them to come over with the night vision (I was still in my tent and had no intentions of venturing out). After a look through the night vision, I heard one of the lads shout: "what the ----! is that," and then the

....and so we find the Hobbit camp (picture courtesy of Andy Williams)

running of feet. Whatever it was shot off down the hedgerow at a fantastic speed. They came back and tried to follow it in the land rover, but were unable to spot it again.

Chris M, who first spotted the eyes, believes them to be have been too low to the ground to have been a big cat. The others who saw the animal disagree. Chris Johnston says of the incident:

"Myself and Andy where in the hide at 1.00am and we could hear the neighbouring farm's dog. It was getting very agitated. I then thought I saw something run across the field, through the night vision scope. We then heard a grunting noise; there where no other animals near to us at the time and this sounded close. A few minutes after this the lads called us to say Chris M had seen something, so we went back to the base. We picked up a set of yellow eyes looking at us through the bushes separating two fields. We waited to see if it came any closer, but it did not. We tried to get closer to it, but when we got there it had run up the field and was looking at us. It had moved very fast in a short time. Steve and I ran towards it while Andy kept an eye on it through the night vision scope; we could not get close, so we got in the car and went round the fields but did not see it again."

After the excitement had died down, myself and Chris Mullins manned the hide at 02.00hrs. It was bitterly cold, and we decided to walk around the area - the fields, farm and lanes - in the hope of catching a glimpse or a sign of anything

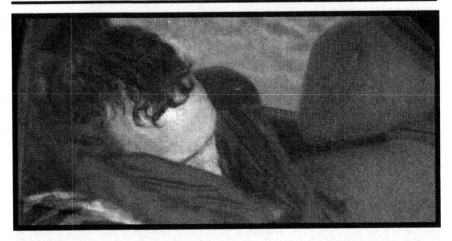

Mark Frazer after a hard nights work! (picture courtesy of Andy Williams)

that could be attributed to a big cat.

The rest of the lads were happily snoring away so we never woke them, but decided to put on a brew. Another disaster - for some reason mine and Chris M's stoves burned very slowly. It turned out that he has the same stove as us and has encountered the same problems. Yet previously to coming down there had been nothing wrong with them at all.

We let the lads sleep and retired to our tents at 05.35hrs, only to be woken up at 06.30hrs by Ade's alarm. My new airbed had deflated, and due to the wrong tent poles the tent was sagging so I jumped out and jumped in the car, turned the engine on and went to sleep for a couple of hours.

James from the BBC arrived at 08.00hrs to conclude the interviews and after that the rest of the lads headed into town for coffee etc.

For the rest of the day, the lads scoured the surrounding fields and farms for signs, but could not come up with anything other then dog-prints.

A photographer from the *Ripon Gazette* arrived and took a few fun photographs, and the rest of the day amounted into nothing much happening. We were beaten by the cold and did not fancy the prospect of spending another night in the tents. At 16.00hrs we began to depart the scene after decamping, and ventured off in different directions for various parts of the country.

The filming by the BBC was part of a series of programs entitled 'Country Cops' which was aired in August. Our piece was edited drastically leaving a fair bit out; they also got our name wrong and put us down as the British Big Cat Society! But all in all it was fairly balanced and quite enjoyable.

FEBRUARY

1st: Yorkshire/England. Dr Steve Hutchinson contacted BCIB after sighting an animal that he could not place while walking his dog on Allerthorpe Common, near Pocklington. It disturbed him because, having a degree in zoology, he should have known what species of cat he was looking at. Steve's wife Lisa also saw the animal. He described as a 4ft long, 3ft high black cat standing in the undergrowth, next to a track

He said: "I was extremely scared to tell you the truth. Even though I have got a degree and doctorate in zoology, what I saw was enough to make my heart go like a trip hammer." The animal was about 50 yards from him when he saw it and it quickly "bounded once and disappeared into the thick undergrowth." Dr Hutchinson reported his sighting to the police who suggested that it might have been a "greyhound or something." "But I know it was definitely feline. The tail was rounded at the end like a ball stuffed in a sock, not pointed like a dog's tail." *(source: Mark Fraser)*

2nd: Dunbartonshire/Scotland. A local Dunbar taxi driver Martin Mchale, and his passenger were shocked to see a five feet long black cat on the outskirts of the town at around 18.30hrs. The driver was forced to brake hard to avoid hitting the animal when it walked out in front of the vehicle near to the entrance of Blackcastle Farm and opposite Totness Power Station.

It was described as having a "long drooping tail" jet-black and was illuminated in the headlights for at least 30 seconds as it simply stopped, looked at the car for and then walked off into a wooded area.

Mr Mchale said: "The guy with me used to work in a zoo and thought it was either a panther or a puma. I have been driving taxis in this area for five years and have never seen anything like that before, " But now that I have I feel very privileged".*(source: East Lothian News & Edinburgh Evening News)*

Early February: Oxfordshire/England. Farmer Nick August spotted the 'Beast of Burford' was quoted in the *Oxfordshire Mail* as saying: "It was at the beginning of February. I was coming from Westwell on to the A40 at about 2.30pm and it was trotting down the road in front of me. "At first I presumed it was a dog, but when I saw it side on it looked like a very big cat, completely black and with a large tail. My mother has also seen it near the farm about 10 days ago." *(source: Oxfordshire Mail)*

4th February 2005: Northamptonshire/England. "I was driving home from work, towards West Haddon, along the Guilsborough to West Haddon road, approximately 0.5 to 1 mile outside Guilsborough when a large black cat walked across the road in front of me and then stopped in the ditch at the other side of the road and watched me as I slowed to look. The time was approximately 7pm. "The cat literately walked across the road, it was in no hurry. It was larger than a medium sized dog but smaller than a large dog, I would say about the size of a golden retriever. It was jet-black apart from a light patch on it's front/chest area (sorry I don't know the technical term). The odd thing is I can't remember whether it did or didn't have a tail. It was definitely a cat of some description. I know this from the way it walked, the shape of it's head/ears and the way it's eyes looked in my headlights.

"For your information, I am a 30 year old Engineer who is not prone to exaggeration and I am normally very sceptical about everything, I definitely saw a large black cat.

I hope this information is useful to you." *(source: BCIB report form)*

5th February 2005: Ayrshire/Scotland. Sighting of a large black cat around the village of Hayhill. *(source:Mark Fraser)*

5th February 2005: Staffordshire/England. "While driving home from Amington, (Tamworth) to Tutbury after collecting my wife from a night out, we turned onto the main road which runs from Tamworth to the M42, and after 1/4 of a mile I slammed my brakes on after seeing a large head, and two glowing eyes, very low looking as if to come out of the hedge. It stared at the car head on, and did not move, but I stopped and changed into first gear, and crawled for about 10 metres, but I had passed the animal, so I sped up the road, and turned around, to come back for a second look. Sure enough it was still there and was watching us for about 1 minute as we watched it. It was very smooth, and very shiny, and appeared to be black with short hair. It was much stockier than a German Shepherd (we have 3, and often see them from the front at night in the dark as we come home) It did not move at all like they do, and its head was much lower to the ground. It looked very muscular, and was moving it's shoulders and neck around almost to get a better view of us!

"The main thing I noticed was that it's eyes were very far apart, and very round, rather than looking like they were on the side of the head. And, it had it's mouth open for the whole duration, and I could see quite clearly it's tongue. It was not anywhere near as long as a dogs tongue, and the face appeared very blunt and squat.

"After about a minute, it turned, and we saw its legs (it was behind a broken fence/hedge but clearly visible through a large gap) It's back leg was very muscular, and thick, and it moved very smoothly away, and into the field. It looked much longer, and heavier than any of our dogs. Two of our dogs are jet black, and we saw them half an hour later when we returned home, and by the difference in size, shape and the way they moved, it was obvious that we had not seen a dog that was on the loose, and it was far bigger than any fox or badger (we are used to seeing these and we would not even consider it being one of these) My wife thought that there were two animals, but I could only see one."

The cat was spotted near Seckington Village at 01.30hrs and described as being black with a 4ft long body and a tail around 1-2ft that curled.

Extra sighting: "About one year ago on our way to the airport during the early morning in the summer. The fields were misty, but it was a lovely bright morning and the sun was out, but it was about 5:am. As we made our way out of our village (Lullington in Derbyshire at the time) I saw a large black animal with a long tail running away from the road in the field. Very fast, with it's tail up in the air with a curl to it. I mentioned this but we could not stop as we were going to catch a plane. I wasn't driving, and got a clear view, for about 5 seconds." *(source: BCIB report form)*

Circa 5th July 2005: Renfrewshire/Scotland. A large black cat spotted by the Knaps Dam. *(source: Greenock Telegraph)*

February: Aberdeenshire/Scotland Many prints found around a small pond near Turiff, measuring 4 inches across. *(source: BCIB report form)*

Exact date unknown, February 2005: Sussex/ England. A 'large cat', similar in size to an Alsatian, was spotted by a security guard at Chandlers BMW. The beast had been prowling around cars in the forecourt. *(source: BCIB report form)*

February 2005: MOD/England. Deer carcass found. *(source: Mark Fraser undisclosed location)*

6th February 2005: Lancashire/England. Witness telephoned Christopher Johnston to report that the dogs he takes for walks have been acting unusual over the last couple of days, around the Formby area *(the coast road near RAF Formby)*.

The dogs, when reaching a certain spot, will stop in their tracks and will refuse to move, very frightened. The man has seen something in the area which he believes to be a lynx.

Alan Fleming reports that at least two sightings of large black cats as big as

Labradors have occurred in this area; one two years ago and the other in 1995. *(source: Christopher Johnston)*

8th: Renfrewshire/Scotland. Jim Bain and his brother-in-law Gordon Hamilton reported spotting a six-foot black cat near Inverkip on the road leadingto the Everton Scout Camp. They watched the animal wandering about gorse for around ten minutes. at around 11.30hrs. Jim said: "It was a lovely morning. There was frost on the ground so the black really stood out."

They described the cat as having a long tail, but could not identify what species it was. The men are not worried about the cat being in the area, in fact its not the first time Mr. Bain has seen it. Last January he saw it wandering fields, again around the village of Inverkip, but no one believed him. He said: "I don't think it is something we need to worry about. They rarely come out during the day. To be honest it doesn't really concern me. I don't think it would come to the houses because it is too noisy with all the children." *(source: Greenock Telegraph)*

10th: Leicestershire/England. "My daughter saw a panther on Thursday 10th February at about 6.15am.

"She was walking along Enderby Road from the Foxhunter Roundabout towards Whetstone. As she walked across Enderby Bridge, she saw the panther in a field to her right. Sometimes there are cows in the field but not that morning. (Could be part of Merrydale Farm?)

"The panther appeared to be crouched low and moving slowly. Its tail was flicking from side to side. *(source: BBCRG report form)*

11th: Renfrewshire/Scotland. Witness on the outskirts of Kilmacolm believes he saw a big cat and taped the noise it was making. The noise has been positively identified by several people as that of a buzzard. The only prints that I and a reporter present at the time found were freshly made dog prints. Yet the witness still believes he caught the sound of a big cat on tape. *(source: Mark Fraser)*

12th: Sussex/England. Security officer Michael Heaysman reported seeing a large black cat "the size of an alsatian," he immediately reported it to Hailsham police.

He said he saw the animal prowling between parked cars while on patrol at Chandlers BMW in Gleneagles Drive. Sgt Jon Scammell, of Hailsham police, said Mr Heaysman had reported seeing a large cat with a very long tail, rounded ears and a small black head. This latest sighting is not the first in the area, after this report was published in the Eastbourne herald two more people came forward and claimed to have also spotted the animal last year in the same area. *(source: Eastbourne Today)*

Circa 14th: Renfrewshire/Scotland. A man and his wife in Gourock herd a very loud noise in their back garden, believed to be like the sound a big cat makes. They have never heard the likes of it before and reported it to the local paper. *(source: Greenock Telegraph)*

Circa 15th: Yorkshire/England. A large black cat was spotted on the outskirts of Walkington in the East Riding. Also large paw prints found. *(source:Mark Fraser)*

Circa 18th: Aberdeenshire/Scotland. A lady living near Marywell, Christ-church spotted a large cat slightly larger than a collie dog. Described as having short legs, tail that tucked under. *(source: BCIB report form)*

18th: Yorkshire/England. I am a part time warden on Hatfield and Thorne Moors in Doncaster. I was walking on Saturday 5th February 2005 and came across some big paw prints so I marked where they were and took a picture but it was a bit to dark to see clearly so I came home and went back early Sunday morning with a tape measure and recorded how big they were. And they measured five and a half inches wide so I took another photo. I am wondering if you could help me with what you think it could be as there has been sightings of a Puma in Armthorpe, Doncaster a couple of years ago. *(source: BCIB report form)*

February 2005: MOD/England. Large black cat seen in darkness. *(source: Mark Fraser undisclosed location)*

19th: Renfrewshire/Scotland. A Renfrewshire resident believed he had found the den of what he calls "Kilmacolm's black leopard". He said: "There is a large flat area where it has been laying down and there is a strong smell of urine which is a dead giveaway. I know it is not foxes because I know that smell." *(source: Mark Fraser)*

20th: Nottinghamshire/England. 1815 hrs. I was driving through the village of Sturton Le Steeple, Notts, with my partner on 20/02/05. We were driving at 25mph as the road was wet and were going north on Cross Street at 1815.

"We were just passing the small Post Office on the right when I noticed a very large black animal on the road ahead. It was running straight towards me, right in the middle of the road. The street was lit but it was very hard to see as it appears to be matt black, apart from its greenish eyes. It was moving very fast and low and was not like any animal I had seen before.

"It got within 10m of the car and turned very quickly to the east, into what appeared to be a drive to one of the houses. As we passed the drive we could not see anything.

I am convinced that this was a big cat, most probably a black panther. I am a zoologist by degree and instantly picked up that this was something very special. It was quite slender when it was running towards us and the speed at which it changed direction could only be achieved by a feline.

"I reported the experience to my partner's mother who indicated that it is common knowledge that big cats have been spotted regularly in Caddy Woods, near Sturton Le Steeple." *(source: BCIB report from)*

23rd: Dorset/England. Wendy and Richard Plummer of Slades Green, Bridport, were driving on the Beaminster road, Meplash, when they turned a corner up the hill and saw through a gap in the hedge a large black cat. She said: "It was two fields away.

"There was nothing else in the field.

"It was 11.35am, the sun was out and it was slinking, like a cat does, hunching its shoulders. It was definitely a big cat.

"Had it been a normal cat we would not have seen it two fields away." *(source: Dorset Echo)*

25th: Ayrshire/Scotland. Email Hayhill. "This morning our neighbour stopped us as we walked our dog back home to say she had just seen a similar animal walk through field just in front of her house (see 5th) heading towards our house about 200 metres up the track. She had time to grab binoculars and get a good look at it and said it appeared to be quite unconcerned, going about its business heading to small wooded area between our properties. It was at least the size of our quite big Labrador. Of course, we looked about but could see nothing. We were rather concerned for our horses and wondered if there had been any similar sightings in the area. We are between Killoch colliery and Sinclairston, off A70 from Ayr to Cumnock.

"Would be interested to hear of any similar experiences in our area. Also do you think these animals would pose a risk to horses - there are farms around with quite a lot of sheep and hares etc so guess food options are not that limited?" *(source: Mark Fraser)*

25th: Dorset/England. "At around 9.00am last Friday morning, February 25th, I was walking my dog up the rough track opposite Knapp Farm, Corscombe; the track leads eventually to the 356 Dorchester to Crewkerne Road. I had not gone very far along the track when I heard the sound of loud purring seemingly coming from the hedgerow. It was far louder than the purr of a domestic cat and I felt half nervous and half intrigued. My dog had continued further up the track and I stayed around for a few minutes quietly trying to see in to and along the hedge. After a couple of minutes the loud purring ceased and all was quiet. I continued the walk and when I got home told my husband. Later that day I sat down to read the *Bridport News* and some headlines jumped out at me - - ' Wild beast of the West back again.'

"I had not seen the beast but it did sound very close and I wondered if the sound could have come from some disused Badger sets around the area, in and close to the hedgerow; it could perhaps have been using them for shelter. There were sheep and I believe baby lambs in fields belonging to Underhill Farm close by, and I feared for their safety.

"I feel certain that all these stories are true because approximately 3\4 years ago my friend and I were walking in the vicinity and we both saw at a distance of about 150 yards the big dark slinking cat that others have reported. This was across fields between Lower Farm and Knapp Farm and it was so much bigger and longer than a domestic cat." *(source: Merrily Harpur)*

27th: MOD/England. A worker was to have his second sighting on this day, his last one was seven and a half years ago. On this occasion he was to briefly see its shoulders and rump, running in a dip between two hills. Jet-black. (source: Mark Fraser undisclosed location)

27th February 2005. Cambridgeshire/England: Sighting by Terry Dye.

"I was going to work (late again) at 14.50hrs today, Sunday 27th February 2005. I was approaching the disused railway crossing just outside Histon, near Cambridge on the Oakington side, when a largish cat ran very quickly across the road from right to left. It had an animal like a small rabbit in its mouth.

"It's body was about 24-30 inches long and its tail about 12 inches curled up. It was long and low. Its colour was grey 'tortoise shell' with white bits in between, and the weather was bright sunshine and a few flakes of snow, "The sighting lasted two seconds. I stopped and followed it into the field but it was soon gone. This area is not far from other sightings in the area and the descriptions match others. *(source: Terry Dye)*

MARCH

1st: Hertfordshire/England. A big cat, believed to be a black leopard was spotted by a Mr Roger Taylor as he was driving a train along the Liverpool Street to Cambridge line between Bishop's Stortford and Stansted at around 4.30pm on Saturday.

The cat was on the west side of the line about 20 yards north of the Michaels Road bridge and close to The Aspens along a track which is used quite often by members of the public.

Mr Taylor said: "I spotted what I thought was a black dog and thought, that's silly, fancy letting it loose this close to the railway line.

"It was about the size of a large Labrador, but when I looked again, I realised, by the way it slunk away close to the ground rather than bounding off, that it was definitely a cat."

He last saw the cat disappearing into undergrowth. There have been several sightings reported in the area over the last few years. *(source: Herts & Essex Observer)*

circa 2nd: Kent/England. Pamela Rolfe spotted a large brown cat in a field near Hildenborough while travelling to London on a train. She said: "The train was going its usual slow speed and I was able to have a good look at it." *(source: Sevenoaks Chronicle)*

1st: Aberdeenshire/Scotland. Doris Moore has finally seen the cat that may have caused her the injuries in 2002. As she sat in her car near Insch she saw a very large, jet-black animal whose hind legs seemed smaller than the front legs. Graceful, it bounded away in one leap, looking at her before it did so. It was bigger than any Alsatian, with straight up pointed ears. *(source: Mark Fraser)*

Early March: Aberdeenshire/Scotland Dennis Johnstone spotted a large black cat near his smallholding on the outskirts of Insch. His wife Dorothy first saw the cat, Dennis said: "For a second she thought it was a normal cat, but it stretched from the edge of the road. across the centre, and the road is six feet wide." He describes the cat as black, two feet tall and four feet long, with a long tail. He continued: "Its a really stocky and muscular looking animal. We told a local farmer about it and he was not surprised. It was a few weeks later in April when Dennis saw the cat himself when motion detectors outside of his house were set off. "It was about 10.30pm and gettig dark," he said: "I went out and there was a big cat sitting on the stone dyke which runs around the outside of the property. All I know is it was not a domestic cat gone wild, and it also wasn't a Scottish wildcat. *(source: Aberdeen Press & Journal)*

Early March 2005: Aberdeenshire/Scotland. The Press & Journal sent the following photograph taken by a lady in the Aberdeenshire area. The witness claims it is a big cat the sizeof a Labrador dog, and that she was standing seven feet away from the animal when she took the photograph.

The picture when (courtesy of the Press & Journal) blown up has the face of a monkey! (source: Aberdeen Press & Journal)

6th: MOD/England. A large black cat spotted sunning itself on a concrete plinth. *(source: Mark Fraser)*

7th: Cumbria/England. 'The Beast of Shap' was spotted by a group of day-trippers from Uttoxeter as they travelled along the M6 towards Orton during the afternoon. Joe Alcock saw the animal in a field by the side of the motorway. He said: "I could see it clear as day."

"It wasn't a normal black cat, it was at least three feet long, which is what caught my attention."

"It was sat in snow near a stone wall about 300 yards away, so I turned to the girl behind me and said that's a big cat, isn't it?' I tried to tell my wife but she didn't take any notice, she probably thought I was joking."

Mr Alcock, previously unaware of any sightings of such creatures in the area was suprised to hear in the New Village Tea Room at their next stop, that it is common knowledge in the area. *(source: Westmorland Gazette)*

8th: Oxfordshire/England. A large black cat spotted on the Westwell to Burford Road. *(source: BBC News website)*

circa 9th: Durham/England. The legendary 'Durham Puma' has been busy this month with a spate of sightings and a savaged deer. Police took the sightings seriously.

Joe Quinn, a greengrocer from Stanley reported in the local press that he saw the creature near the Northumbria Riding School, past the Jolly Drover roundabout, on the Consett to Stanley road while delivering flowers during the heavy snowfalls that the area experienced. He said that because of the snow the outline of the cat was very clear and added: "It was massive. At first, I thought it was a big dog but, as I got closer, a Shetland pony came to mind

"There was no mistaking the fact that it was a cat." The cat then bounded off the road and ran across a field.

Two days earlier and only half a mile away at Iveston a deer was killed, believed to be the victim of a big cat. Police Sergeant Eddie Bell said: "A farmer saw the cat chase the deer over a fence into a bit of woodland and kill it. They went up later and found a deer carcass, which had a bite in the front of it which appears to have been the way it was killed. "It is probably a cat because it had to get near the deer to attack it.

"It is easy to tell the difference between a dog and a cat killing and we have recovered droppings from cats in the wilds of the North-East."

Margaret Richardson of Good Street, Stanley, reported finding "massive prints in the snow" that led from her house towards Beamish Woods. "It must have come next door and hopped over the fence then took off across the green in front of the house," she said.

"The prints were so big they cannot have been human and they were about a yard apart.

"It must have been a big cat. It is quite worrying that they can come so close to home." (source: This is North-East) circa 10th: Hampshire/England. Several sightings of a large black cat around the village of Liss. *(source: Diss Express)*

14th: MOD/England. Deer carcass found that had been stripped clean in 45 minutes. *(source: Mark Fraser)*

15th: Pembrokeshire/Wales. Dixie Tilley was cycling along roads on the outskirts of Haverfordwest when he spotted what he thought looked like a "black panther." He got to within 40 yards of the animal getting a good look at the animal before it slinked away under a fence.

He told the BBC: "I thought, oh that's a big dog. I was cycling quite quietly, then it saw me and went under the fence. It sort of loped across the field and I thought, that's not a dog," he said.

"I could see by the shape of its tail. We've got a cat at home and it's just like it, only this is 20, 30 times bigger. But it seemed to cover lots of ground, then it sort of disappeared."

"It was jet black and it was really, really shiny. It was bigger than an Alsatian but longer.

"If you see a cat, their back is flat and their head is low. A dog is more upright and a tail is swishing.

"I don't know much about them really. I've seen these stories in the paper and I've always taken it with a pinch of salt really, but having seen it, it's wonderful. "It was out of the blue - a minute, minute and a half and it was gone. It would be nice to see it again." *(source: BBC Radio Wales)*

circa 15th: Oxfordshire/England. Farmers in the west of the county claim that the so-called 'Beast of Burford' has been recently responsible for killing sheep. Farmer Colin Dawes from Foxbury told the BBC that he saw a large black cat running away after killing three of his sheep. One expert reported on the BBC News website that "the sheep were killed with the typical big cat hunting technique. "It grabs them by the throat, strangles them and then rips out their throat before taking away the front shoulder."

Now the Cotswold Wildlife Park have offered a £5,000 reward for its capture (the press does not say whether this means dead or alive). Richard & Judy also offered £1,000 for photographic evidence.

Wildlife crime officer PC Ray Hamilton based at Thames Valley Police said that there had been several sightings lately and added, "We've had sightings of everything you could imagine - pink flamingos, lions, dingos, wolves and even a giant ant-eater in Pangbourne.

"I keep an open mind, I have to, but I do think people mis-identify things.

"Something is killing sheep. I don't know what that is, but there is a possibility there's something out there, an animal that shouldn't be there, but I don't have any proof." The Cotswold Wildlife Park director said that the big cat could not have escaped from the park and that it was more likely to have been released. After the reward by the park a picture came to light that was taken by a regular at the Masons Arms pub in Brize Norton. Phil Buck of Carterton waited with a camera early one morning after Landlord Dave Fleming told the Oxfordshire news that he had seen the animal. He said: "I saw it in a field near the pub. It was about the same size as a Labrador and at first I thought it was a dog. It wasn't until it moved and I saw its ears and tail, I realised it was a cat."

Mr Buck said: "The picture was taken during the harvest and the piles of hay in the field were about 2ft high. It was a lot bigger than a domestic cat and the way it moved looked a lot more powerful." *(source: BBC News & This is Oxfordshire)*

The picture now hangs in the Masons Arms for all to see.

17th: Sussex/England. Harry Marshall while out walking his dogs at 18.15hrs spotted a large mysterious black cat. He said: "At first I thought it was an enormous black fox but then I realised it was too big for a fox."

"It was walking very purposefully and when I got within 40 yards of it, I called to try to attract its attention. *(source: Midhurst & Petworth Observer)*

21st: Sydenham/London, England. Anthony Holder had an horrific experience with what is claimed to be one of Britains' mystery big cats during the early hours of the morning in south-east London.

Mr Holder had gone to his back door to call in his pet domestic cat when the incident occurred. He said: "Just before 2am I was trying to look for the cat. I heard her crying so I went to the bottom of the garden, which is quite over-grown, to try and find her.

"She sounded in a bit of distress. Then I saw what I thought was a fox on top of her but it wasn't - it was a big black cat about 3ft tall and 5ft long nose to tail."

The cat then lunged at him knocking the ex-soldier to the ground "I am 6ft and weigh 15 stone and it was considerably stronger and bigger than me. This thing was huge," he added.

"I could just make out our cat under another animal. "I kicked out at it, gave it a good boot.

"A split second later it leapt on me and sent me sprawling on my back in the bushes.

"I couldn't roll it off me. It was mauling me with its claws and making this terrible hissing and snarling cry.

"Its huge teeth and the whites of its eyes were inches from my face. I was terrified and fighting for my life.

"I was grappling with it for a good two minutes before it ran off."

Tony was left with a 5 inch scratch on his face, a cut wrist and his finger had been bitten. While this was going on his 11 year old daughter Ashleigh watched from the bedroom window. She said: "I just saw my dad flying backwards and struggling with something, I was really scared."

After managing to fight off the animal he raced into the house and called the RSPCA. They advised him to ring the police, who then turned up with an armed response unit. One of the officers also saw the cat-like animal and described it as being as big as a Labrador (other reports suggest that what the police officer did see was actually a Labrador). The police, armed with taser guns, then sealed off the area before conducting a search, but failed to find the animal.

Police issued warnings for people in the area to remain calm, vigilant and to stay away from wooded areas. Local people took the incident seriously and on the following day school gates in the area were locked and folk were avoiding the more quieter parts of the area. *The Guardian* reports that 16 year old Ben Mumford said that his local school were not allowing young people out alone and had issued warnings over the loud-speaker system.

"They told us that we hadn't to go to the woods, or go down any alleyways," he said. We had to stay in a group and make a lot of noise." Some parents said they would be keeping their children indoors.

Tony Holder's sighting was not the only one that morning, by the afternoon it had been spotted three more times, once by him again. As he was being treated by paramedics they all saw it "saunter past". How and where the papers do not elaborate. Police also said that there had been similar sightings two years ago in woods nearby and that this was the third serious incident of a big cat in London during the last three years. Three hours after the incident at 05.00hrs painter and decorator Billy Rich, who lives not far from the incident, was looking out of his bedroom window when he saw "this thing." He said: ""It was big and black and I thought, f***** hell, what was that?

"It definitely wasn't a pussy cat. It was too big. The way it jumped, you could tell it wasn't a dog. It definitely wasn't a fox, but it can't be a panther - where would a panther come from in Sydenham?"

Tony's wife Joy said: "He was wonderfully brave." *(source: BBC News/ Evening Standard/Daily Mail/The Guardian/Greenwich Mercury)*

21st: Kent/England. "Hi there I live in Sidcup, Kent. I am not sure if this is relevant or not, but I am walking distance from the station, around 4min walk. "Anyway a couple of years ago my husband did not have a sighting but heard what he believes to be a large animal growling at him in the early hours of the morning. Well my husband leaves for work around 4.30am in the morning when it is still dark. One morning he came out of the house and heard something down the side of our house growling at him. He couldn't see anything, but the growl was enough to convince him that he had heard some sort of large cat. He said that it made the hairs on his body stand on end and that he was terrified and therefore made his way swiftly towards his van, and off to work. Nobody believed him, and generally laughed at his experience. I did believe him as he hadn't been drinking the night before and on his return from work he immediately purchased a security light for the area in which he believed the animal had been located. "My sighting was a few days ago, 12.30pm (lunchtime) on Monday 21st March 2005. I had just gone out into the garden to peg out some washing. I must have been on the second garment when I heard the fence which was behind me moving. I looked around but never noticed anything as I have quite a lot of shrubs and trees in front of it, obscuring the fence entirely. I believed it to be the trees leaning against the fence. I turned back to continue pegging out the washing and again heard a noise. I then heard movement at the end of the garden, as I turned my head to the left to where I heard the noise, I noticed something leap up and over my 4ft fence. The thing was black and it happened extremely quickly, the movement as it leaped over the fence appeared to be that of a cat, and the size of a dog. Initially I thought 'Fox', must be. What a black fox that leaps? Then, maybe my black dog 'Max'. No way, my dog didn't leap like a cat. I recalled what I had seen again - yes it had leaped within a small space, kind of vertically over the fence. "I ran into the house and told my husband who was dozing in the front room, he instantly believed me, but wasn't going to look over the fence where I said that big cat had gone. "I made a call to the RSPCA, I explained what I had supposedly seen, and the lady on the line reassured me that I wasn't going mad and said that there are many around the country. She then gave me another charity wildlife number to call. The lady I then spoke to was very informative. We chatted for a long while, she took my details and that was that.

"The next morning around 7am, I had Capital Radio on, instantly on the news it was announced that there had been a sighting by two men in the early hours of 22nd March (around 2am), seeing what was described as a big black cat the size of a labrador dog. Apparently one man was attacked in his garden and called on the police, the policeman was apparantly the other man.

"That morning I telephoned the lady from the charity organisation again, and she said that she was happy to collaborate my story if needed. I then called the police and left a message on the mobile of the policeman involved in this incidence, I also contacted the RSPCA who apparantly were dealing with it. Who then said that they knew nothing. No one has contacted me back since. (source: BCIB report form

Date unknown: Oxfordshire/England. Sighting of a large black cat around Chipping Norton. *(source: This is Oxfordshire)*

22nd: Lanarkshire/Scotland. A large black cat walked out in front of a motorist near Barrhead. Officers described the man as a credible witness, but found no trace of the animal - said to be the size of an Alsatian, but closer to the ground, with a metre-long tail. *(source: Barrhead News)*

23rd: Peterborough/England. Andrew Leatherland, while walking at Castor Hanglands spotted one of Britain's mystery cats, and said: "I was walking down a track, when, about 150 yards ahead, I saw a jet black shape. "It was about the size of a large Alsatian and walking on the left-hand side of the track.

"I was fascinated and scared at the same time. "Thankfully, it was walking away from me, and I don't think it picked up my scent.

"It was just ambling along and went round a bend, and I didn't see it for a bit.

"I couldn't believe it. I phoned a friend of mine, who told me to be careful.

"Then I saw this black shape just walking on slowly across a piece of grass-land." He added: "Its shoulders were hung low, and it had cat-like movements - it was definitely not a dog." *(source: Peterborough Times)*

24th: Lanarkshire/Scotland. A large panther-like cat seen by Glasgow City Council employees on the golf course in Linn Park. One golfer was said to have seen "a big cat, a big black panther" close to a rubbish bin near the parkland course's tenth hole, but initially chose to remain silent in case of ridicule.

However, after a sleepless night he reported the sighting to a park supervisor. A second golfer later made a similar report to staff. *(source: Paisley Daily Express)*

25th: Lanarkshire/Scotland. A large black cat sighted on Linn Park golf course. *(source: Paisley Daily Express)*

25th: Hampshire/England. Chris Jenkins, Landlord of the *Bluebell Inn*, Farnham Roam in Liss, saw a large black cat-like creature while driving home He said: "I realised I was looking at a big cat and it was totally black. I am sure it was a cat. It did not move like a dog." *(source: Diss Express)*

25th: Renfrewshire/Scotland. Whilst driving out of Kilmacolm this evening at almost exactly 7pm, heading towards Port Glasgow, a large black cat ran across the road approx 10 feet in front of a car. It was about 3 feet tall with a long, slimline body and a small head. It was jet black. It had appeared from behind trees on the witness' right, around 100 metres past the entrance to the cemetery and ran into the field on his left. *(source: Mark Fraser)*

circa 25th: Gloucestershire/England. A young blackbuck gazelle was attacked and killed in The Cotswold Wildlife Park, believed to be a victim of a big cat.

Experts say that the creature that killed the blackbuck, and that also left prints behind, killed in a fashion typical of big cats. *(source: Western Daily Press)*

28th: Aberdeenshire/Scotland. Photographs showing what is clearly a domestic cat were sent in from the Elrick area. *(source: Mark Fraser)*

29th: Renfrewshire/Scotland. An unnamed motorist reported to police that a "panther-type" cat had walked out in front of his car on Aurs Road in Barrhead at approx. 01.45hrs. Police immediately searched the area but found no trace. *(source: Glasgow Evening Times)*

APRIL

Various dates: Highland/Scotland. A large black cat has been spotted several times on crofts around the Lochaber area. It has been described as more "than four times the size of a domestic cat". It has also been seen by the father of Liberal Democrat leader Charles Kennedy. One crofter believes it has been responsible for killing more than a dozen of his poultry over the last 18 months.

Ian Kennedy, who owns a croft at Lochyside near Fort William, claims he has seen the animal a number of times. He said: "We have seen it from about 80 yards and it is like a large cat, but with stumpy ears and a broader face than a normal cat, and three to four foot long from nose to tail. It sits on its haunches like a dog for half-an-hour at a time, just waiting and watching, then speeds off," said Mr Kennedy. *(source: The Express).*

Exact date unknown: Yorkshire/England. A dead deer had been savagely attacked and was discovered by walkers on Allerthorpe Common, believed to be the victim of a big cat. *(source: Pocklington Today).*

2nd: Warwickshire/England. Rowington villager Julie Abrahall was on her way to work at 8am on Saturday morning when she saw the puma-like animal jumping into a hedge just a couple of metres in front of her, on the road to Lowsonford. She told the Herald: "All I saw was this thing going through the hedge. Its back legs were black and very muscley - there is no way it could have been a domestic cat. It was probably the size of a cocker spaniel." *(source: The Stratford Upon Haven Herald).*

2nd: Norfolk/England. A cast of a paw print at a site, which has now been sent to the Natural History Museum in London for identification, has prompted fears the carnivore may be living in Diss and on the prowl.

Henry Haggard had a lucky break in tracking down the panther which came early one morning as he made his way past the Mere's Mouth and spotted what he believes to be a large black creature near the far end of Madgett's Walk.

Judging by the size of its paw prints and the photograph he took, the creature is approximately 5ft to 6ft long. "I believe the photographic evidence speaks for itself.

"I tracked the creature to its lair - I'm keeping the location a closely guarded secret - and took the casts. These paw prints definitely come from a big cat." *(source: Diss Express).*

3rd: Suffolk/England. 08:00, Being a regular listener on a calm morning of the big cats at Kessingland Wildlife Park, I was amazed to hear the exact noise coming fron the opposite direction as normal, estimated 2.5 miles away. (Sorry, I live at Wrentham 3 miles due south of Kessingland) The wind was WSW at the time and I know it was a big cat. Do Black Panthers make a similar noise as a lion, because if not we have something else out there a little bigger. The black panther has been seen on a regular basis here for the last 3 or 4 years, most recently on a local shoot where that was more than one observer. Bigger than a lab, thick tail to match and not tapering. Also lynx has been seen on my farm 4 or 5 times in the last two years. *(source: Via email to Chris Moiser).*

3rd: Cumbria/England. Location not known. "I had a call today, the person was in deep forest in the Lake District. They saw quite a few lambs that had been killed by some animal. I know there have been some sighting in the area as someone has a clear photo of a black cat but will not let me see it. He definitely has it as others have seen it. *(source: Christopher Johnston).*

4th: Surrey/England.

Time: 6:00pm

Location: Brooklands, Weybridge.

Brooklands was a race course and an airfield, it is now partly developed and partly wasteland.

Height, length, length of tail, shape of ears: Black, same size as a greyhound but a much sturdier build. Long tail that swooped down to the ground and curled back up again. Rounded ears.

Although Weybridge is not exactly what you'd call the countryside, it is home to St Georges Hill, a massive housing estate to the rich and famous; many of these properties were home to wild cats in the 60's.

The cat has been sighted by 3 of my other family members independantly over the past 4 years in exactly the same place. I never believed them until now! The cat sits and walks along the remaining race track which runs vertically around Brooklands, it is flanked one side by trees and over growth and the other side by the main road.

It's difficult to explain but the high side of the track stands as high as a house and is almost vertical then it curves steeply down so that the bottom side runs along the road.

I sighted the cat, sitting at the top of the track. Initially when I saw it, it was sitting down, very relaxed with it's back legs laying flat and lifting it's upper body on it's front legs. It looked at me and had a very feline face with bright eyes. As I drove past it got up and walked towards the shrubbery.

That's when I saw the size of it and the length of it's tail, it also had raised shoulder blades and it's back dipped a little (making me think of a greyhound). But it most definitely looked and moved like a cat, slinking rather than plodding as a dog would do.

The animal was in no hurry. My mother father and sister all sighted an animal fitting the same description on the same length of track during daylight hours on different occasions. *(source: BCIB report form).*

circa 5th: Sussex/ England. Reverend Ron Jones spotted a large black cat which he described as 'bigger than an Alsatian' while walking his dogs in fields off the Cuckoo Trail near Hailsham. He said, "He was looking straight at me. He was sitting around 40 metres away from the hedge. He looked at me and I looked at him, then after a couple of minutes he sloped off..... this was definitely a panther."

Mr Jones bases the opinion on having seen leopards while on military duty around the world. The incident was reported to the police. *(source: Eastbourne Herald).*

5th: Northumberland/England. Firstly, I'm really not sure that what I saw was a big cat, but at the same time I'm wondering whether it might have been. About 30 minutes ago from now, I was walking my dog through fields in Northumberland. It's a rural area and from where I was standing probably a mile from the coast. I was walking along the tree-line at the top of a hill; below at the bottom was a dip, a cluster of trees underneath a railway embankment. I was immediately aware of "something" standing at the bottom of the hill. It was sandy brown in colour, but standing in the sun a definate red tint to its body. It appeared to be standing motionless, looking straight up the hill at me. I stood for about 60 seconds trying to work out in my head what I was seeing, at first I thought it was a fox because of the colour, but it seemed too big - I've seen foxes from a similar distance before and this must have been the size of my dog at least, a border collie. I clapped my hands to try and get it to move, but there was no movement so I decided to approach it to see; I called the (completely uninterested) dog and started down the hill, at which point it darted off through the trees and towards the railway. I could see from its movement that it was quite long, had a long rounded tail and it moved quickly and effortlessly out of sight. My head says it must have been a very large fox, but there's enough doubt in my mind to contact you about it.

The time of the sighting was 15.50hrs, the location was fields/woodlands along-side a mineral line. The animal was standing in the corner of a field surrounded by the woodland at a distance of 75 yards away, and motionless.

The witness continues: " It was looking directly at me. Had its side to me, but was definately looking up the hill. As I approached it, it darted into the trees. Reddish brown in colour. With the sun shining on the animal it had a definite red/orange glow to the side of its body. When it ran into shade it looked reddish brown all over. The tail was long, quite thick and with a rounded end. Carried straight behind it as it ran."

Length of the animal was 3-4ft, height 2-3ft. The witness is not sure on the length of the tail, but it did have "pricked up ears".

The witness continues: " My head says it was a big fox. But there was some-thing weird about it, I have seen foxes before and was always 100% certain that that was what I had seen. This time, there's an element of doubt in my mind and I'm sure there has to be a reason for it.

"This is more of a query than a definite sighting. The way the animal behaved and the way it looked struck me as odd, while all the time I'm trying to rational-ise what I've seen by thinking that it had to be a fox...if I'd seen it in Devon or Cornwall I might have been much more inclined to think that it was something weird, but this part of Northumberland doesn't exactly seem like ideal big cat country. Does the look/behaviour sound more like a fox? I'm not sure what to make of it. The silly thing is that on days like this I often take my digital camera out with me, and would have had plenty of time to photograph whatever I saw before it ran off, or film it. But today I didn't have it with me. I don't think my dog even noticed what I saw, he was too busy urging me to carry on with the walk! Thanks for your time. *(source: BCIB report form)*

6th: Fife/Scotland. "Ian let our dog out at approx 10.30pm at our home in Aberfeldy. The security light went on, and he saw a very large cat running out of the garden. He knows the size of it, as our small Labrador tried to chase it. Our dog measures 20 inches to the shoulder, and he reckons the cat was about 2 inches taller. The dog's tail is 15 inches, and the cat's tail was about half that length again.

It turned to look at Ian; it had short hair on its face, but the rest of body had long hair. Its tail was very bushy almost like a fox's tail. The whole cat was ex-tremely sleek and very glossy, as Ian said, "It was in really good nick". When it turned to Ian, he saw it had yellow slits for eyes. We hope this is of use to you, and if we have any more sightings, we will be in touch. *(source: Kay Gordon).*

6th: Essex/England. Three chickens, three ducks and a cockerel were eaten in a night and Kelly Green was sure the 'Beast of Essex' was responsible. The next evening she stayed awake all night in the garden at Mersea Road, Langenhoe. Her efforts paid off as when she entered the garden after hearing a noise she came upon a large black cat 20 yards away. She said: "I startled something. I would say it was something like a panther. It was a huge black cat. It jumped over the fence and into the field." *(source: Evening Gazette).*

7th: MOD/England. Roaring, snarling and struggling sounds. *(source: Mark Fraser).*

8th: Highland/Scotland: I have just had a call from a friend about a big cat. An animal was taking chickens from an allotment in the highlands of Scotland, so they put a trap out to catch what was doing it and caught a black cat. The animal was 20 lb and jet black with a long tail.

The person who owns the allotment did not want the cat shot and it was released, but it came back and they caught it again. Sadly this time it was shot and they buried it. He is going to try and get the body for us, as this happened only in the last few days. *(source: Christopher Johnston).*

9th: Northhants/England. The witness was stood at the Northampton train station at 15.13hrs when he reports seeing a large black cat, which he identifies as a puma. It was stood about 40ft away from the witness and was about 2-3ft in height, 4-6ft in length. The witness reports that a watchman also saw the animal on a previous occasion. *(source: Mark Fraser).*

11/12th: Hampshire/England. Petersfield resident Steve Whiting of Inwood Close saw a large black cat while driving home late at night. (source: The Petersfield Post).

12th: MOD/England. Another deer carcass has been found, with 2 ½ inch prints alongside it. They were the best prints I have seen so far, yet we are unable to bring them off site. *(source: Mark Fraser).*

circa 15th: Co Durham/England. Andrew Spence found 12 of his lambs killed in horrific circumstances. *(source: Unknown).*

15th: Highland/Scotland. Christopher Johnston reports hearing about an alleged catching of a large cat in a cage near or in Kincraig. Nothing else is known. *(source: Christopher Johnston).*

16th: Cwmbran/Wales. A picture of what was said to be a large leopard appeared in a national newspaper. Not many people that I have talked to are convinced of the picture's authenticity. The story, I believe, is as follows: Norman Evans was conducting a model photo shoot in a remote forest above Henllys Village in Cwmbran, South Wales, when he claims he stumbled across the animal 15 feet away from him, happily tucking into a pigeon.

Chris Moiser and Paul Crowther's reconstruction.

Norman said, "I couldn't believe my eyes. I was in total shock. My nerve went and I was shaking like a leaf, it looked like a black-panther straight out of The Jungle Book. It was fully grown and really healthy, eating its lunch about 15 feet away. I walked away quickly, and said to Hayley, get in the car and lets get out of here. Once I got in the car I showed her the picture."

Model Hayley Evans said, "Norman looked white as a sheet. It's scary to think a panther is roaming around in an area where kids play."

Mr Evans reported the incident to the police and he later returned to the area and found the remains of feathers scattered everywhere but no signs of the big cat. Police confirmed that there had been several reports of a large black cat reported in the past months around the Cwmbran area, and John Partridge of Bristol Zoo said: "the image on the picture suggests a black panther fully grown."

More confusion reigns; Danny Bamping, founder of the British Big Cat Society is quoted in the paper as saying that this is definitely a leopard, as is another re-searcher from the west.

Chris Moiser, after studying the photographs, sent the following report to the national newspapers:

"I worked for 20 years teaching Biology. I have written '*Mystery Cats of Devon and Cornwall*' (published 2001), '*Big Cat Mysteries of Somerset*' (published March this year), and '*When the Cat's Away*' (a novel about the beast of Ex-moor) which will be published later this year. I have in addition, whilst studying wildlife visited The Gambia (13 times), Zimbabwe, Zambia, South Africa, and Botswana. Having seen the photo and report as published in your paper it is my opinion that:

1. The picture shows a toy that is commonly available in street markets etc. for about £20.00 (It is a nice toy!) The shape of the head although roughly accurate is slightly too long in the face. Secondly, the bends in the tale are not consistent with a real tail and the bend near the body, even if the result of a fracture, is too sharp and too near the body for a real wild animal.

2. If the animal was a genuine wild leopard (a black panther is just a black leop-ard), Mr. Evans would not have got within 15 feet of it - the animal just would not have let him.

(source: The Sun - Chris Moiser - The South Wales Argos - Wales on Sunday).

Exact date unknown: Yorkshire/England. A dead deer which had been sav-agely attacked was discovered by walkers on Allerthorpe Common, believed to be the victim of a big cat. (source: unknown)

17th: Northhants/England. Large black cat seen by four cleaners at the Northampton train station. *(source: Mark Fraser).*

18th: Cumbria/England. Holidaymaker Eileen Leah, 52, says she has seen a brown lynx twice while staying in her caravan at Priory Road, Ulverston. She said, "I saw it both times while walking my dog and another woman staying at the park also saw it with me." *(source: Westmoreland Gazette).*

circa 20th: City of London/England. Laura Downes, 47, of Westmount Road, Eltham, discovered a dead fox in her back garden and thought nothing more of it. An hour later when she went back outside there was nothing left of the fox except clumps of fur scattered around the garden. The following day another dead fox appeared in her garden; this time its head was missing and it was covered in maggots. Laura said, "It had been dead for several days and there was a hole as big as my fist in its neck, squirming with maggots." Only a big animal would have been capable of jumping her fence, she reported to local newspapers. She called in animal expert Eddie Williams of Willow Wildllife. He said, "It was horrendous. Whatever did that to the first fox did a good job. I've never seen anything like it. I was scared." He was unable to discover what had killed the foxes, although he is sceptical of big cats on the loose. *(source: This is London)*

Circa 20th: Oxfordshire/England. Phil Batts, of Thorney Leys, Witney, took a photo of what he believes could be the animal's paw print in countryside near the perimeter of RAF Brize Norton. Mr Batts said, "It's too big for a fox and it wasn't one of my dogs, so unless it's a huge dog like a Great Dane I don't know what it is."

Mr Collinson, of Sturt Close, Charlbury, said he believed a cat could be living wild in the area, but says the print is inconclusive. He said, "It's possibly a cat, but it's not certain. What I'm looking for is whether there are any claw marks. If there are it's most likely to be a dog, as cats have retractable claws. *(source: Oxfordshire Mail).*

20th: Kent/England. Oakwood Park, Maidstone. Mid Kent College, Kent Institute of Art and Design. Security guard Richard Stephens was on patrol when he saw the big cat in a car park at about 1am on Wednesday, April 20. Mr Stephens, from Gravesend said, "It was a drisly night and I was going to return to my hut but decided to check one specific area. As I rounded the corner, under the glow of the car park lights stood a black cat, around 6ft in length, with fur like velvet."

Mr Stephens said the animal glared at him, crouched down and bolted up a bank. The cat had a long tail and stood 2ft at the shoulder. Mr Stephens followed it, but it disappeared into the trees. Mr Stephens added, "I wasn't scared of the animal which is why I followed it. It appeared to be healthy and quite young." *(source: This is Kent).*

20th: MOD/ England. Large jet-black cat seen. *(source: Mark Fraser).*

20th: Lancashire/England. A couple saw a big black cat in a field near to their home in Preston at 19.00hrs. It was playing on bales of hay and kept jumping on and off. The cat was 3ft high and 6ft long. *(source: Mark Fraser).*

20th: Highland/Scotland. Yesterday. My husband and I went for a walk from the dam at Loch Mullardoch (Glen Cannich) to the top of 'toll Creagach 1053m'. It was a sunny, slightly hazy day, with a cold windchill. Attached you will find some pictures of the big paw prints (8cm across) that we found in the snow patches at the summit. I am assuming they did not belong to a dog, as there were no human prints to be found anywhere at the top. We have been wondering what the prints are - possibly those of a big cat, maybe even two as the 'run around' prints seem to show two animals chasing each other, or perhaps playing or mating. Could the prints be from a native cat, its paw prints enlarged by stepping in the snow? Or might we have witnessed the prints of something much bigger?

We did not really look for other clues, but our imaginations started to wander as we descended the hill - especially after 20 minutes or so when we found the antlers (head and backbone attached) of a deer, with some skin still present. The two might not have been connected, of course, but then again the deer could have been the kill of a big cat. Pressed for time, we did not stop to look for other clues.

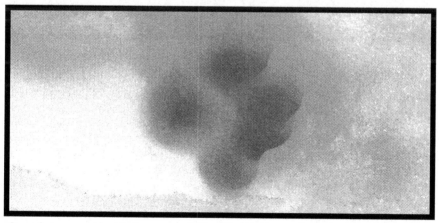

Once home, we decided to try and identify the paw prints via the internet and came across your site. Can you help us to identify the prints? If of interest to your site, then you are welcome to use them. *(source: Mark Fraser).*

22nd : Lancashire/England. A farmer saw a black cub walk across a path and then into woodland. Three cubs have been seen here over the last few months on the outskirts of Preston. *(source: Christopher Johnston).*

22nd: Northhants/England. Railway workers spotted a large black cat crossing the lines at the Northamptonshire train station. *(source: Mark Fraser).*

Roebuck carcass in Eggerslack Wood

23rd: Cumbria/England. "On 23rd April 2005 I came across the remains of a Roebuck in Eggerslack Wood near Grange-over-Sands, Cumbria (grid ref SD 410 785). The animal had clearly not been dead for long, but much of its carcass had been stripped to the bone. I could not imagine what might have removed such a large quantity of meat in a short space of time. I took a photo, which I have since discussed with a couple of mammal experts. Both of them suggested that it could have been the work of a big cat. A quick Internet search showed that there have many reported sightings of big cats in Cumbria, though none of them were from the Grange-over-Sands area." *(source: Mark Fraser).*

Exact date unknown: Lancashire/England. Have just heard that another cat might have been shot in Lancashire. I will be in the area tomorrow night to investigate. *(source: Christopher Johnston).*

24th: Wiltshire/England. "As we were driving out of Avebury in Wiltshire I spotted a black animal bigger than a large dog which I think was a black panther walking in a field. I could tell this wasn't a dog by the way it walked. This was around 7.30pm." *(source: BCIB report form).*

24th: Gwynned/Wales. Police have issued a warning following sightings of a panther-type cat roaming Dwyfor. A local farmer, Ynys Pandy, at his holiday accommodation at Golan saw a large black cat moving in undergrowth. He said: "I could not believe my eyes and picked up binoculars to make sure it wasn't an illusion or that my eyes were playing tricks.

What I saw was amazing! The animal was very big, bigger than a dog, black and had a very long tail. It walked across the land like a cat; low down and very stealthy, and moved into marsh land at the bottom of the field. It was a very impressive creature and I called my wife to take a look - she had no doubts either and we watched it for a few minutes. There have been lots of sightings so there's something out there." Remains of a half eaten sheep were found nearby. *(source: South Wales Argos).*

24th: Oxfordshire/England. Stephen Thompson of Wantage Drive found a dead Canada Goose in his back garden, possible the victim of the big cat often seen in the area. He had heard of recent accounts of a large black cat stalking sheep in the Lambourn area and wondered if the incidents are connected. The goose had its head taken clean off.

But Graham Scholey, conservation team leader for the Environment Agency in Wallingford, said it was more likely that a domestic dog was to blame. He said foxes were capable of killing fully-grown domestic geese but did not usually do so in residential gardens during the day, and that it was unlikely that a mink or polecat would take on a Canada goose.

Mr Scholey said there was no reason to suggest there was a rogue predator at loose in the area.

Mr Thompson saw the large black cat on his drive way three months ago. *(source: This is Oxfordshire).*

25th: Cambridgeshire/England. Nene Valley railway, Peterborough.

Hi all. We have been getting reports of a panther sighting on the NVR at Wansford, Peterborough on Monday evening.. A NVR volunteer was working in a coach in the station when a panther-like big cat walked past at 10 feet away! The report is second-hand but from a reliable source.

The whole station and tunnel are on CCTV remote monitor, but only when the station and sheds are not occupied. However, as the cat is often seen here I have asked the GM to let us know if they get any CCTV footage. Interestingly, we had a report 40 miles west of there that day, at Peckleton near Leicester. *(source: Nigel Spencer).*

25th: Leicestershire/England. "I live in Peckleton and had a sighting yesterday morning at about 8.30 am of what I can only describe as a black panther. I was about 150yds from it, travelling out of Peckleton towards the Caterpillar factory when I saw it come out from the right hand side of the road. It ran quite quickly across the road and in through the bushes on the left. It ran like a big cat, and was quite big with a very long black tail. It was definitely not a dog as its head was very much the shape of a cat. There is local knowledge of the Peckleton panther but I was not aware of this until last night. *(source: Nigel Spencer).*

26th:Hampshire/England A large cat-like animal has been sighted by two people at different times on land off Wylde Green Lane, Liss. *(source: Petersfield Herald).*

27th:Hampshire/England A large black cat sighted at Steep Marsh near Liss. *(source: Petersfield Herald).*

28th: Lanarkshire/Scotland. "A black cat has been seen prowling the grounds of a local country park and golf course in Scotland. Descriptions we have so far are big and black. Curiously, a couple have said that it has a low or curved stomach. Could be pregnant, or just prowling. I am hoping to head over at some point today, and try and speak to the green keeper who has seen it. The word on the street is that it has been seen on Lynn Park golf course just next to the park, several times in the past 8 weeks!! The manager of the golf course has seen it, and says it was big and black with a low tummy. *(source: Brian Murphy).*

29th: Kent/England. Photographs of prints taken at Tenterden. *(source: Nigel Spencer).*

30th: Yorkshire/England. Driving to Harrogate today on the A59 eastbound about 7 miles from Harrogate, I saw a Big cat walking up a field along a wall away from me. It was a jet black cat very large with a long tail that was turned up at the tip. The cat was about the size of a large dog. It was walking along slowly.

I saw the big cat at around 10.50am. The weather was clear with no rain and I had a good view of it for about 3-4 seconds as I was a passenger in the back of the car. The cat was fairly large about 4ft in length without the tail. It definitely looked like a black panther and not a household cat. The tail was almost as long as the main body and was being held fairly high with it turned up at the tip. The tail also seemed fairly thick as compared to a normal cat. *(source: BCIB report form).*

30th: Fife/Scotland. "Thought that you might be interested in this. My husband and I were travelling towards Dundee from Glenrothes. Just past Fernie Castle on the left hand side I saw a very large black cat padding through a field towards a wooded area. My husband didn't see it but offered to turn the car around. I'm sure there wouldn't have been any point as it was quite close to the woods and by the time we turned around it would have been gone. It was larger that a dog and was most definately a cat. I could tell by the way that it moved (I have a cat myself). This would have been around 12.30pm on Saturday 30th April. I have to say I was quite shocked as I have always been a bit sceptical about these 'sightings'. Not anymore! *(source: BCIB report form)*.

MAY

1st: Surrey/England. Dogs chased a large cat-like animal up a tree near Whitmoor Common, Guildford. *(source: Surrey Advertiser)*

1st: Somerset/England . After several sightings of a large black cat in the Weston-super-Mare area, farmer Mark Penfold reported to the *Western Daily Mail* that he believed a large cat was responsible for an attack that killed one of his young calves on his land near Hewish.

The farmer said that he had never seen an animal so thoroughly devoured in such a short time before. Recently, while out lamping rabbits his light caught a pair of eyes that he did not recognize; he said, "What I saw down the end of the lamp that night was something else, I have seen deer, badgers, rabbits, hares - I know what animals are out there - but not this."

Mr Penfold also found a large print, which he says was on a different scale to that of his large dog, a bull mastiff-American pit bull cross. "His footprint doesn't come anywhere near it," he said. Five other friends also saw the curious mark.

Shortly afterwards he found a flock of his neighbour's sheep huddled in the corner of a field, apparently terrified in a "way that he had not seen before." Mr Penfold has never seen the animal, apart from the eyes, but is positive that there is something out there. It's just that he is not sure what, exactly. *(source: Western Daily Mail)*

2nd: Yorkshire/England. Mr A. believes he spotted a lynx at close range while investigating bell pits near Wharfedale. As he approached one a biggish cat got up, looked at him, walked over to and entered an adjacent pit. This was from a distance of 10-15 metres away.

Description was 3-4 times the size of a domestic, but very well-built; reddish-brown in colour with rough hair and no obvious tail.

The witness said that the legs were short, which doesn't fit lynx unless it was slinking away. When he got up the courage to look into the bell pit that the animal had gone into, he found that it had disappeared, but that there was a hole at the bottom of the pit. He feels that this may be were the cat lives. He doesn't know anything about cats and has subsequently scoured the local library for info on cats and feels that it most closely resembles a bob-cat.

After passing the message on to Christopher Johnston, he hotfooted it over to Yorkshire to meet the witness. After viewing the area Chris feels that this is not a home for the cat, but that it was merely out hunting in the area. *(source: Mark Fraser)*

circa 3rd: Somerset/England. A large black cat has been spotted around Lower Wear near Axbridge. *(source: unknown)*

circa 4th: Dorset/England. William Willoughby spotted what he believes was a lynx from his living room window, only yards from a playground in Weymouth. He said, "I came downstairs for a cigarette and opened the window. As I looked out – we have good street lighting here – I saw what I first thought was a fox. It was obviously a lynx, three times the size of any normal cat.

"It snarled up at me three times and I thought it was going to attack so I pulled up the window a bit. It stayed there for a good four or five minutes, I think it may have been cleaning itself. Then it jumped onto the back wall, which is a good 6ft high, and then into the back garden."

Mr. Willoughby described it as a lovely looking animal. It had mouse-coloured hair and big eyes like a domestic. After the animal had left, three domestic cats came and began sniffing at the spot where it had been stood.

As fate would have it, Mr. Willoughby had turned off the CCTV only days before! *(source: Dorset Echo)*

4th: Linn Park, Lanarkshire/Scotland. Thursday 21.00hrs, a worker cycling along the path leading to the main car park on the Linn Park saw a very large cat run out of the bushes, across the path and onto the golf course. Said to be as big as a Labrador and carrying a pigeon in its mouth. Said he knows the difference between a cat and a dog. *(source: Brian Murphy)*

7th: Linn Park, Lanarkshire/Scotland. Print found, photographs and a cast taken.

Heel pad = 2 and three quarters

3 and a half inches in length 2 and three quarters width. *(source: Mark Fraser)*

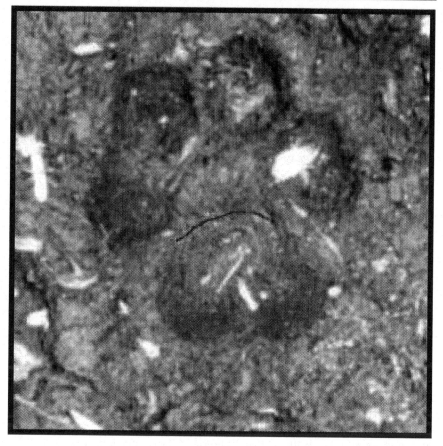

Print found in Lanarkshire, Scotland

The 'Beast of Lytham', Lancashire. A strange beast has been reported more then 20 times by worried locals, leading to the artist's impression (right), based on these eye-witness accounts. Not a big cat by any means, others say it's a mangy fox; whatever it is, it's now dubbed the 'Beast of Green Drive'.

It is described as about as tall as a collie dog with huge ears, a large mouth and a lolloping gait. The animal has caused quit a stir in the district of Lytham St Annes. It is spotted mainly in the large wooded area of Green Drive where there is plenty of cover for it to get lost.

One witness, Sandra Sturrock, said, "I caught sight of something large ahead of us. It was like a large collie, light in colour with large stick up ears. It was watching me and my dog. I stood completely still for several minutes trying to see it more closely. I called my dog and put him on the lead and slowly inched towards the animal to get a better look but it ran off."

Willie Davison, a painter and decorator in the area, said, "I was playing bowls near Green Drive when I heard a snarl behind me. It was like a monster out of Dr. Who and it needs tracking down."

Another woman, on encountering the animal, described the experience as "surreal", and described it as big as a Labrador.

A local police spokesman said they had checked local zoos and nothing was missing. He added, "It is very bizarre, we have handed it over to the RSPCA to investigate." *(source: Lancashire News)*

8th: Northamptonshire/England. Maria Harding and her seven-year-old son came face to face with a large jet-black cat, described as a panther while out walking at 2pm in the afternoon. They were in a park between Clannell Roan and Rowtree Road in East Hunsbury when the terrifying encounter took place.
Mrs Harding said, "There's a park which is opposite Tesco. We went into the wooded part and my youngest son asked me 'Is that a dog?'. We saw this animal behind some ferns. It was very big. It was too big to be a cat. It certainly wasn't a dog. You could tell from the way it moved off that it was some kind of cat. It was scary. I thought it was very strange. At the time I couldn't believe what I was seeing. I couldn't work out what it was."

When they spotted the big cat, which was smaller than a German shepherd dog but bigger than a fox, they were about 10 feet away from it. They then tried to follow the animal but lost sight of it in some bushes. *(source: Northampton Chronicle)*

8th: Dorset/England. Another sighting of a lynx has been made in Weymouth, not far from William Willoughby's sighting earlier in the month. This time it was seen by Westham residents in the home of Terry Smith. She said, "I had visitors round, I was tired so went to bed, they stayed up, they told me later that they had seen a large cat hanging around which looked suspicious." *(source: Dorset Echo)*

9th: Staffordshire/England. Nigel Taylor (47) saw the 'beast' not far from his Warton home as he travelled to work at 9am on May 9 in the Warton/ Polesworth areas.

He said, "I was driving past a field there was a gap in the hedge. There, fifty to a hundred yards away, I saw a large black cat. Nose to tail it was between four and a half and five foot long and around eighteen inches of it was clearly visible above the long grass. It was unmistakeably a big black cat. I have seen a large animal in the same area before. That time it was dark but the animal had green eyes, and I'm quite certain of what I saw." *(source: unknown)*

Circa 9th: Gloucestershire/England. A large black cat has been spotted around Woodmancote, Badgeworth and Leckhampton. It is described as being a metre in length, with a small head and a long tail. Mary and Jim Alison believe the cat is responsible for decapitating their pet cat *Tigger*.

Local big cat investigator Frank Tunbridge said the cat spotted in these areas is most probably the one and the same as they fit the same description, although he does state to the *Gloucestershire Echo* that he believes that are 500 big cats lose in the British countryside.

John Blenkinsop said he saw the 'beast' along Stockwell Lane towards Cleave Hill at 7pm when he noticed something moving on the footpath to his right. He said, "It looked like a cat, only much bigger. It was about 3ft high. It slinked past a fence and then disappeared."

Huw Philips of Stackpole believes he may have solved the riddle of the large black cat often spotted in the area, after finding the carcass of a dog otter which measured 41.5 inches in length with a girth of 26 inches. He said: "I have never in my life seen an otter this size. It would have been nearly four feet tall when stood up on its hind legs." *(source: Gloucestershire Echo)*

10th: Yorkshire/England. There have been three reports of a large black cat in the Meltham area of Huddersfield. A woman went into her back garden just before 6am as she had been alerted by a noise; she then stared in utter amazement at a very large black cat swiping at a bird's nest, trying to get the chicks inside. The cat then turned to look straight at her, growled and then slinked off into the early morning light. Several police officers scoured the area in an unsuccessful attempt to find the animal.

Farmers in the area talk of lambs being ripped to pieces, and believe it to be the work of a large unknown predator. *(source: Huddersfield Daily Examiner)*

circa 10th: Dorset/England. 80 year old Joyce Ash of Tollerdown Road said she saw a big cat from her kitchen window on an empty garage forecourt at the top of Benville and Chickerell Roads. She said, "I thought it was a fox at first, I watched it for about ten minutes. It was the size of a big dog and it went off down Tollerdown Road. It was certainly a big cat and seemed to have a long tail with a big tuft on the end. It was very ugly looking." *(source: Dorset Echo)*

11th: Borehamwood/England. A swan was found up a tree on Berwick Road by six-year-old Carl Parker and his mother. 50 meters from the tree sits a spot where it was likely killed, before being dragged or placed in the tree. Residents in the area believed it had been killed by a large panther-like cat and then taken up into the branches to be devoured, especially after Danny Bamping stated that this was a great possibility.

After the carcass was taken away for post-mortem examination, RSPCA officer

Jill Sanders said "I've never seen anything like this before. It's odd that it's up there in the first place. It could have been foxes if there were four or five of them - especially if a vixen has young.

"The only puzzling point is the tree. I would like to be able to put people's minds at rest and say it was foxes, but how did it get up the tree?"

A week later, after the commotion had died down, local resident Allan Ziff came forward and said that he had actually found the swan several days earlier, and suspecting foul play he informed the police. Mr Ziff dug a hole to bury the body, which may have been dug up later by foxes, and then thrown into the tree by youngsters or pranksters. *(source: Borehamwood Times)*

11th: Leicestershire/England. Via Nigel Spencer. Just got report of large black cat, 1 ½ feet tall (standing above second bar on farm gate) very heavy set head, large paws and strode purposefully. Watched witnesses as it walked away. Seen near the quarry by a husband and wife at about 40 metres away at closest point. Bardon is about 1 mile from Coalville and Thringstone and about 2 miles west of M1 j22. *(source: Nigel Spencer)*

14th: Lancashire/England. Farmers near Preston spotted a large cat in the fields near their farm. They did try and take two photographs, but we have not yet seen the results. *(source: Christopher Johnston)*

15th: Rutland/England. I have just seen a large cat on the road between Oakham & Tilton at Withcote. It was about the size and build of a greyhound with a long tail of constant length fur. It was walking slowly on the right hand side of the road & then stepped in to the verge & disappeared Its colouring seemed to be very dark brown as opposed to black, and I could tell from the way it was walking with its rear shoulder blades moving up & down that it was a large cat, and not a dog. *(source: Nigel Spencer)*

15th: Lincolnshire/England. 7.30 pm on remote country lane between Bolingsbrooke Castle and Miningsby. Spotted big cat walking along side of road at a long distance, was not sure what it was at first. When we drove closer it was clear that it was a large black cat, long thick tail, turned up at the end not far from ground level.

No markings, just black, like a Puma. Size, 3 to 3.5ft long more with tail. Possibly 2.6ft tall maybe a little more. We got fairly close in the car, the cat turned and disappeared in thick verge/hedgerow. *(source: BCIB report form)*

15th: Yorkshire/England. A large black panther-like cat has been spotted in New Mill by two parents taking their children to Kirkroyds Infants School. Both are adamant that it was not a large domestic cat or a dog which was yards from the playground.

In light of recent sightings the *Huddersfield Daily Examiner* has offered a £500 reward for photographs of the mystery feline. *(source: Huddersfield Daily Examiner)*

15th: Surrey/England. Video footage was taken at Winkerton Arboretum by a Mr Harry Fowler which shows a Labrador-sized, sandy coloured animal walking along a path in the bright afternoon sunshine.

Mr Fowler said he was standing on the Azalea Steps when a woman nearby pointed out the animal, which was walking away from him towards Phillimore Lake, near the boathouse. On the video you can hear the woman say, "It's huge! It's walking like a cat" before she cuts off. Mr Fowler describes the animal as gingery-brown in colour, about the size of an Alsatian dog and "definitely not a fox." He watched it for a good minute and a half from a distance of a 100 yards. He passed the film onto Surrey Wildlife Trust Ranger Mark Havler, who said that it was difficult to make out exactly what it is. Although the *Surrey Advertiser* reports that Mr Havler believes it could be a Spanish lynx, the tail is plainly visible

A still from video footage of a large cat-like animal taken by Harry Fowler of Guildford at Winkworth Arboretum, Godalming. *(source: Harry Fowler: Picture courtesy of Harry Fowler)*

17th: Yorkshire/England. The cats seem to have a thing for schools this month, especially in Huddersfield. Just two days after the sighting near the Kirkroyds Infants School, Judith Morris spotted the panther-like animal near Linthwaite Clough Junior. She said, "We often walk that way because the field is full of rabbits," said Judith who was going to the school to pick up grandson Damon, six.

"All of a sudden I saw something move very quickly and the rabbits all scattered and ran down their warrens. When we looked we could clearly see the cat - it was huge, far too big to be a domestic cat or a dog. It was prowling across the field. My daughter was petrified. She was trembling and we certainly will not be walking across that field for a while now." *(source: Huddersfield Daily Examiner)*

19th: Bexley/England. Jim Hornby spotted the now famous 'Beast of Bexley Heath' at 23.00hrs when at work just off Bexleyheath Broadway. He said, "It was some time between 11pm and midnight. I was in the utility room at the back of the building and standing next to the open door, which leads onto the car park and then onto woods.

I was chatting with the night superviser when I saw something out of the corner of my eye, moving in the car park.

I turned and saw the shape of a big black cat, creeping along the ground on its belly by the side of my car, as if it was stalking something.

It was much bigger than an ordinary cat, a fox or even a dog."

The next morning large prints were found in an area of sand measuring 5 inches across the depth, reports the *London Shopper*, indicating that something heavy made it. *(source: News Shopper - London)*

19th: Dorset/England. School teacher Pat Marsh may be the latest to spot what locals think is a lynx. She was walking in the St Andrews school grounds at Preston with a friend when the animal appeared in front of them. The time was 20.15hrs. She said, "It came out of a hedge and trotted along in front of us for a few yards, then disappeared back into the hedge. We both said 'wow, it's a lynx'.

It had a small head of cat proportion, short ears and neck. It had cat-proportioned legs and was ginger brown in colour." It did have a tail she added, but is not quite sure if lynxes have tails or not. *(source: Dorset Echo)*

19th: MOD/ England. Large sandy cat-like animal spotted. *(source: Mark Fraser)*

22nd : Dorset/England. Dorchester resident told the *Dorset Echo* and the police that he saw a tabby cat "twice the size of a large Labrador with pointed ears" in Allington Avenue late at night.

The animal glared at him before scaling a wall and disappearing into the night. *(source: Dorset Echo)*

23rd: South Downes/England. I just thought I would report seeing a large ginger cat (size of a Labrador) peering through a style at my dogs (black Labrador with 10 week old puppy) and I. This was on Monday afternoon 23rd May 2005 in South Downes. It was about 30 yards away and we were approaching the style. I could not see its body but it's head was looking straight at me and was unmistakably feline. There are lots of sheep with lambs in the fields here Meeting with the local farmer yesterday he showed me a lamb he had just found with it's whole insides gone and its ribs bitten through. The lamb was quite fresh and clean. He had lost another the same way a week ago. By the time I had crossed the style with my puppy, my Labrador had presumably chased after the cat to the other side of the field and was running about excitedly. *(source: BCIB report form)*

26th: County Monaghan/Irish Republic. A large black cat was seen on the outskirts of Monaghan Town. *(source: Charlie McGuinness)*

27th: Buckinghamshire/England. We were walking our dog across farmland/ industrial estate at approx 21:10 between Horsenden and Princes Risborough when we saw in the distance on the path what we thought first of all was a stray dog, it was motionless and staring straight at us. As we got nearer approx 25 metres we realised it was a type of black big cat with a small head and ears and long tail it was about two feet high with a body of about four feet long. The cat suddenly ran off in to the woodland as we approached nearer which is when we noticed the long tail. We were quite shocked to have seen it and thought we should report it to someone. Strangely before we sighted the cat, my dog had picked up the scent of something and was acting in a very nervous way, unusual for him as he is quite a gutsy jack Russell. *(source: BCIB report form)*

Circa 28th: Dorset/England- Merrily Harpur reports: A man contacted me with this photo, taken this week near Wimborne in Dorset. Two of them watched a panther-like animal - initially static -wander up a field and into the hedge. They were approx. 100 yards from it, and before it disappeared he had time to take a photo of it walking away. *(source: Merrily Harpur)*

28th: Norfolk/England. Richard Porter of South Wootten, West Norfolk, spotted an animal that he said looked like a black panther in undergrowth beside Watling Road near Watling Estates at around 1840hrs. He said, "I saw the animal's back end, from its shoulders backwards. It had its front quarters in the undergrowth and had a big, black, long curved tail.

Big cat sighting near Wimborne in Dorset

I spoke to the estate's head gamekeeper on Sunday afternoon and he said he saw it three years ago.

This was not a dog. I have lived in the country all my life and I've never seen anything like this before. It was jet black and looked bigger than a cheetah."

This sighting even brought a quote from Bob Engledow of Operation Big Cat who retired two years ago. He said, "There's no doubt about it, these animals are roaming around the country. When we carried out Operation Big Cat, there were four cats either resident in West Norfolk or passing through the area. *(source: Lynn News)*

28th: Co Tyrone/N Ireland. A motorist on the Ballygawley Road near Dungannon spotted a light brown cat measuring 4ft in length and 2ft high. *(source: Emigrant online)*

28th: Co Tyrone/N Ireland. A motorist on the dual carriageway near Moygashel spotted a large brown cat, the second sighting within twelve hours. The police say it may be no more dangerous than a wildcat. *(source: Emigrant online)*

29th: Surrey/England. 21.15hrs, Shere Forest nr Bookham Surrey/In the dusk, it appeared to be completely black - a few seconds earlier, in the opposite direction I saw a roe deer, it's russet colour was completely discernible despite the dusk, so I'm not mistaken regarding the colour. Lower than a Labrador, but longer I'd say. It was 50-60 yards off, and I couldn't discern a tail nor ears. It appeared almost 'shaggy' in appearance and appeared to 'scurry' quickly across a forestry track I had just walked down, disappearing into conifers. I was out stalking, so was observant of the wildlife, with all senses switched to high - I'd swear that this creature was conscious of me and was seeking to avoid being spotted by quickly scurrying across the path. I had sight of it for c1 second. There's a house about 500 yds away and the owner has a wolfhound - not what I saw. The next house is well out of range of a domestic dog, but this didn't look like a dog. Badger? nope - different movement, no white on the pelt. Boar? never seen one before so don't know, but boar have a distinctive high back, which this didn't. *(source: BCIB report form)*

29th: Argyll & Bute/Scotland. A Kilchrenan resident was on the Inverinan - Dalavich road last week and slowed down for what he thought was a deer, only to see, when 75 feet from the creature, that it was cat-like.

According to the man, the animal was four feet long and had short, upright ears. *(source: Shaun Stephens)*

May, ongoing: Yorkshire/England Wildlife photographer has had several encounters with what he believes to be a black leopard in the Nafferton area. He has not yet managed to take a photograph of the animal but is making every effort to do so.

Several sheep lost in this area and blame has been put onto the mystery feline. *(source: BCIB report form)*

JUNE

1st: Dorset/England. I was walking my dog and had just got back to the car this evening at about 8:30pm when I saw a large coloured cat in a field of immature wheat/barley.

It was running in leaps and bounds towards a copse. The crop is about three feet high so it must have been a largish cat. It certainly wasn't moving like a dog and had a long tail. It was about three or four hundred yards away from me but didn't seem to have seen me. Driving away from that spot I noticed near the copse a field with some horses in it. I usually walk my dog down that road which is a quiet narrow country lane with minimal traffic, just East of the village of Burton, near Christchurch, Dorset. I was going to report it to the police, but decided not as they are pretty stretched as it is, and they probably wouldn't believe me anyway. *(Unnamed witness source: Merrily Harpur)*

4th: MOD/England. A large black cat seen by support workers from a TV film crew. We were on site only hours afterwards for a night's vigil. (source: Mark Fraser Undisclosed location)

6th: Argyll & Bute/Scotland. John Bakes of Waterside, and his wife were awoken at around 5am on Monday morning (June 6) by the sound of deer barking outside their home. Mr Bakes looked out of his window and saw a large wildcat, which he thinks could be the animal a number of people have spotted in Kintyre over the years.

Mr Bakes said that while the animal was unmistakably a wildcat with a long striped tail, when it moved away from him it looked black from behind. He said that the animal was about 16-18 inches in height and three feet long. John even managed to capture some video footage of the cat stalking a mouse. BCIB representative for Argyll & Bute, Shaun Stevens, contacted Mr Blakes and secured a copy of the footage. Here is his report:

Follow up after a visit made to Mr and Mrs Bakes at their home on Wednesday 15th June BY BBCRG Argyll & Bute representative Shaun Stevens.

After speaking with them it appears that several neighbours have seen the cat on numerous occasions since the beginning of the year. Only two weeks ago two tourists nearly ran over a "large black cat", just outside the entrance to their home. A neighbours' elderly cat has also disappeared recently.

They have regularly seen paw prints and spoors, and heard screeching at night. They are going to film and photograph any future sightings for us and wherever possible take casts and photos of any prints.

Both the gentleman and lady are keen naturalists, the lady being a member of a badger watch at a previous address. The have seen otters, mink, fox and roe deer on their land and in the river that flows in the small valley beside their house. They have also spotted rare butterflies. So I feel that they are excellent, knowledgeable witnesses.

The sighting was made about 5am from an upstairs window. They watched the cat for about 5 minutes before thinking about video recording it. In the video you first see the cat from a distance the camera zooms in. The path the cat walks up is about 2 foot across.

The cat stops at a step, which measures 8 inches high. The cat spots a mouse or vole run across the path (probably a vole because the couple say there are lots of voles in the bank there) and bounds after it. The cat covers the distance between two steps in two bounds. The distance between the steps is just over 6 foot.

The cat then jumps into the long grass after the vole. The grass was about 2 foot high at the time, and you can see the striped tail clearly waving about. They have a very large pet cat themselves, which measures about 12 inches at the shoulder. Taking all these measurements into consideration, I estimate the cat to be about 18 inches high and a body length of about 30 inches. About one and a half times the size of their very large cat. From the size and the markings I have no doubt that it is a Scottish Wild Cat. The cat has the distinctive striped tail, dark stripe down its back and smallish head compared to its body. All of which are distinctive characteristics of the wild cat. The lady contacted the Scottish Wild Cat Trust, who told her "It couldn't be a wild cat, because they don't exist that far south, but could they see a photograph anyway". She wasn't very happy with their attitude and won't be contacting them again. She is more than happy though, to deal with us on any future sightings instead.

The videotape is excellent evidence in my opinion. They are happy for their names to be linked with the tape and any stills you can get from it, but would appreciate it if you could give their location as just Southend, Argyll.

They've had a couple of 'crank calls', including one from a hunter. They have only spoken to me about this sighting in depth. *(source: Shaun Stephens)*

8th: Yorkshire/England. (3 sightings) A large black cat, described as "panther-like" was seen on three separate occasions on Wednesday June 8.

A visitor to Alfreton Park, Ripley, reported seeing the creature at 1.30pm, followed by another sighting in the same area. Later the same day, a motorist said they saw the large cat while driving past Ormonde Fields Golf Club in Codnor. Police say reports described the animal as about the size of an Alsatian dog, and "large and bulky, vastly bigger than an average cat". (source: Ripley Today)

10th: Aberdeenshire/Scotland. A large black cat seen near Pitcaple Quarry. *(source: Mark Fraser)*

10th: Norfolk/England. It was on Friday 10th of June and I was on the road to Kings Lynn in Norfolk to investigate the big cat sighting at Watlington by a gamekeeper on the estate. He had also seen it 3 years ago. At the time there were a lot of sightings in the area around the south of Kings Lynn in the villages of Winch, Congham, Wormegay, Shouldham and others.

Having started on the road at 03.00am, I had been to quite a few of the sites and was now on the approach road to Shouldham Warren - a vast area of woods and open ground, and also where I could get a mile off road. All the usual wildlife were there including partridge, French partridge, wood pigeon, pheasant, crow or rook, rabbit, hare, deer, duck and jay. As I was driving down the track at about 25 mph a large animal came out of the hedge on the right at about 30 yards away. As it seemed to see me out of the corner of its eye it broke into a 'canter', 'loped' (?) across the road in a slow and lazy fashion, and seemed to dive under the fence on the left. On closer examination I found there to be no obvious gaps under the fence and no sign of the cat. The fern grows about 4 foot high around there and I saw the cat no more.

The description is about the size of a slim Labrador dog, domestic cat type with a tabby or tortoiseshell pattern and a deep reddish brown colour, the like of which I have never seen before, not even on a domestic cat. Ears were short (I couldn't see if they were pointed or not), tail was long but not excessive as in a leopard. Tail also held out straight and 45 degrees to the ground. Short cat face and the legs seemed a bit on the thick side. Overall it was nearly 3 foot long and 18 inches high. Tail about 18 inches.

It was across the road in 3 strides. Road was narrow and about 14 foot across. Conditions were sunny and 06.50 am. I looked around for about and hour and then left for home feeling very tired and pleased that I had picked the right place at the right time - or was it just coincidence? I shall be going back soon. *(source: Terry Dye)*

11th: Cumbria/England. I received a telephone call from a gentleman called Martin Offer who, with a friend, found a small cutout in the side of a hill. They said, "we found some very unusual poo, it was too big to be a fox or a badger, or any other animal in the area. There was some fresh and some old, very dark in colour and smelly. *(source: Mark Fraser)*

circa 11th: Dorset/England. Large cat-like prints found in the Dorset country-side. *(source: Merrily Harpur)*

14th: MOD/England. Large black cat seen. *(source: Mark Fraser location undisclosed)*

16th June 2005/Cornwall. Christopher Johnston and various members of the BCIB research group visited Bodmin, and the spot where the 'leopard' was photographed on the wall at Minions in March 2004: see below

(Source: Mark Fraser - the witness who took the photograph wishes to remain anonymous).

THE VISIT

We went to Langage Farm to meet the manager and he showed us the photographs of the cow that was attacked. It looked like something had tried to take hold of the cows mouth area and there where claw marks on the face and neck of the animal. It was hard to see anything other than a cat doing such damage.
There have been sightings in the area of a big black cat for the last 14 months,

and two employees saw it. One of them ran towards the cat but as he approached it, the animal cleared a 6ft high hedge.

At Minions we put the cuddly toy on the famous wall, with interesting results. We tried but we could just not get the toy in the same position as the animal on the original photo; if we put the head facing the direction in the original the body position did not match. We spent some time there and we have taken some photos of what we did.

It may be a different type of toy - I have only seen two available in the spotted cat, my one and the black type in Chris Moiser's photos. We saw the black one and that would not go into the right position either.

Steve and I visited Nigel Brierly on the way down and he gave us a copy of the report that went with the photo and I have attached it. Nigel has talked to the gentleman who took the photo and he is a Policeman and was visiting his dad who lives in the area. Nigel is convinced this is genuine.

We have heard that the occupants of the house directly next to this wall are regularly seeing cats, but we did not know the colour. There have been two more sightings of a cat seen in exactly the same place on the path, described as black and brown.

I think our photos do look like a cuddly toy, but am unsure about the original. If

you look at the tails on the photos, our cats tail just hangs down; on the original it does not, and the end is turned up showing a white area on the underside of the tail The tip of the toy tail is all black.

I think this could be a real cat, but it is interesting that we all have a different opinion.

We also found a dead sheep, about a mile from the location of the cat photo. However, the animal could have died of anything, and then been eaten by a number of different creatures. It is impossible to say for definite what happened.

Chris Johnston's reconstruction.

We put the trigger cameras up, (my pictures are all of sheep.)

What I should have done is measure the stones and also the distance between the stones where the animal is laying to get a accurate size, as well as just putting a toy there. Will do that when I am there again.

Andy noticed that on the original photo the animal does not look as big as the toy, and a friend has said it could be a any variety of smaller species.

Andy Williams on the moor

We were shown just how easily these toys can be mistaken for a real cat. Steve was positioning the toy on the other side of the wall and was out of view, myself and Andy were standing on a part of the path that is set back, so we too where out of view to anyone approaching from our right. A gentleman came along and saw the toy on the wall and turned back the way he had come, he must of thought it was real. A lady also came along and stopped, but then saw myself and Andy, so carried on. I don't know what she was thinking when she passed three grown men with a cuddly toy, but can only imagine. *(source: Christopher Johnston)*

18th: Shropshire/England. Rachael Lowe, 19, of Bridgnorth, said she and her family were sat in their garden at about 6pm on Saturday when they saw a large black cat-like creature behind their Brook Hollow home.

She said the family were convinced it was no ordinary cat and now they wonder if anyone else saw it.

"My dad thought it was a lynx or something", she said. "It looked like a cat but it wasn't your average domestic cat. I think a puma was seen in Shrewsbury a few months ago, so I don't know if it is connected to that." *(source: Shropshire Star)*

19th: Gloucestershire/England. Pauline Saunders, who lives in Kingsmead, Watermoor, Cirencester, had just seen her postman son off to work when she caught sight of the mysterious creature. Through her half-opened door she watched a mysterious cat stroll along a row of cars under the light of street lamps before disappearing into the darkness.

Pauline said: "It came from under a car over the road and was at least four times the size of a normal domestic cat. I was watching it with the door open a bit. It just sauntered down the middle of the road as if it didn't care where it was. It wasn't quite as big as a panther but at least four times the size of a cat. It was quite frightening - it gave me goose pimples." *(source: Gloucestershire Echo)*

19th: Cambridgeshire/England. On Sunday Morning I was walking my 3 dogs in fields behind a housing estate in Chatteris, Cambridgeshire when about 60 meters in front of me a large Black cat walked across my path and into the overgrowth. The size was too big for a house cat and its head was very distinctive also its tail was thick , long and very S shaped.

The size was about 2' long, about 1' tall, very Black shiny coat with a long thick tail which was longer than its body length very distinctive S shape curling up at the end. Its face/nose was larger than a house cat much like my Boxer dogs. It walked with a flow as if it was staying low, straight back with shoulders moving.

Follow-up by Terry Dye.

Last Sunday (19th June 2005) a Chatteris man was walking his dogs (Two Boxers) and next door's Labrador at the bottom of a housing estate on the edge of Chatteris, Cambridgeshire. There is a ditch and hedge then an open strip of short grass, but mainly wild land the width of the field and about 30 feet across, followed by the field of peas which are about two feet high. The field is very big as fields go. Open country beyond that to (I think) the East.

The dogs were running loose in the peas (without the farmer's knowledge of course) when at about 60 meters in front a large black cat walked slowly out of the field across to the ditch and hedge. That is, from right to left. Whether the dogs disturbed it or not, it did not seem to be pursued. Time was about 06.50 Sunday Morning.

Description was Labrador size, about 2 - 3 foot long plus the tail, cat, black. Most noticable was the tail which was long and thick and in an 'S' shape, pointing downwards then curling up. The man could not say anything about the shape or size of the ears, and did not see the eyes. The cat went into the hedge and was seen no more. His workmate suggested that he report it as there were children on the nearby estate who could be harmed. He reported it to the local police who laughed at him. I didn't.

I went with him to the site on the 26th June and we looked around. There were no footprints, due to the weather drying up the ground, save for one dog print which was for some reason "near perfect". I could not search the whole pea field by myself, and it looked very dry. The man along with his family and friends are now looking out all the time and will report any more sightings to us.

The last sighting that was reported to me was a puma like cat (brown) in Doddington which is a couple of miles to the North. *(source: BCIB report form & Terry Dye)*

20th: Ayrshire/Scotland. Prints found in South Ayrshire thought to belong to a big cat. The witness also reports, "A friend has reported twice seeing a very dark, long tail disappearing into dense forestry near his home. Although not photographed, the distance between front and rear prints was some 49.5 inches." *(source: Mark Fraser)*

24th: Ayrshire/Scotland. I was stopped by a Scottish Gas employee in the town to be told of his recent strange sighting. It was evening and he was near Sorn in Ayrshire (I know the spot he means) when a very large, strange looking cat ran across the road about 50 yards in front of him. It was sandy in colour, about two feet in length and 18 inches high, or thereabouts (although the witness asked not to be quoted on size etc.). Sharp, upright pointed ears, with black tufts. A tail as long (maybe a little shorter) as the body, trailed behind in a U shape before rising again off the ground. At the end was a "ball", and the witness clenched his fist to demonstrate the size.

This area has a rich history of sightings, usually black but we have had several reports of sandy coloured cats around here before. *(source: Mark Fraser)*

24th: Dorset/England. At 8.45pm this evening (Friday) my wife and I were driving along the road from Tarrant Rushton old airfield towards Witchampton. At one point a large, all black cat bounded from the left hedge across the road in just two long swift leaps and through the opposite hedge. We must have been 100 feet away, but both of us saw it clearly. It was of muscular build and clearly agile. The size, from the distance we were away, appeared larger than a domestic cat.

We stopped the car and, standing on a bank, could see something black (now probably 125 yards away) searching between standing crops and the hedge. Two horses in a nearby field had seen it, and with their ears up were looking across to the same spot. *(source: Merrily Harpur)*

25th: Shropshire/England. Police are appealing for information after two animals were injured in Church Row, Rowton. A horse and a goose were injured at two separate addresses. The horse was found with a five-inch long slash to its head on June 25. On July 1 a goose was found with an injury to its wing. Possible victims of a big cat. *(source: Shropshire Star)*

25th: Lancashire/England. Screams, likened to those that a puma would make, were heard on the outskirts of a farm near Preston. This area has seen many sightings in the past. *(source: Christopher Johnston)*

25th: Yorkshire/England. A large black cat spotted along Elland Road in Leeds near the football stadium. The man, who wishes to remain anonymous, said, "I was walking along Elland Road and just happened to glance over the wall into the car park, and there was this large furry animal. I didn't get the clearest of looks at it because it was getting dark, but when it ran off at a fast pace, I thought to myself, 'United could do with pace like that on the flanks.'" It later turned out that these sightings were a hoax! *(source: Leeds United press office)*

26th: Gloucestershire/England. Bob Austin, chief executive of Cotswold District Council, spotted a jet black panther-like beast close to his Stratton home on Sunday morning, near Cirencester.

The creature was prowling near children's playing fields on the corner of Grange Court. Stratton has a lot of green open space adjacent to residential property, exactly the kind of location where previous sightings have occurred.

Mr Austin said, "I am absolutely certain about what I saw. It was about the size of a Labrador but definitely not a domestic cat or dog. It was about 75 yards away and this cat-like animal was right on the corner of Grange Court and the open play area. It was standing absolutely still with an arched back and for a moment I thought it might have been a prank, but then it dropped its back, turned in a circle and walked towards the primary school. I didn't follow it because it was bigger the my dog and I thought it wouldn't be a good idea - it was about two feet high and four feet long, with a thick tail." *(source: Gloucestershire Echo)*

28th: Lothians/Scotland. Evelyn MacRae, 53, spotted a large black cat in the back garden of her home. She said: "I was going to close my curtains for the night when I saw this shape.

I knew it was too big to be a domestic cat. It was crouching down beside my pond about 15 feet away from me. It was a hot night so perhaps it was looking for a drink. I found it quite a frightening experience so I stayed inside."

She added, "We only live about 100 yards away from Rosslyn Chapel and there are lots of fields round about us."

Mrs MacRae, a housekeeper, lives in Wallace Crescent, which is not far from an earlier sighting of the so-called 'Beast of Roslin'. *(source: Edinburgh Evening News)*

30th: Hampshire/England. A carpenter working on a building site reported a large black cat loping across a field 200 yards from where he was standing. Adrian Hill, 54, was working at the Bovis Homes building site in Bluebell Way, Whiteley, yesterday morning when he saw the creature, which he claims was up to 1.5 metres long and had a long, thick tail. It emerged from woodland at the bottom of Bluebell Way before strolling slowly over to a pond in the field. Mr Hill, of Barton Drive, Hamble, said he and two other workmen watched it in disbelief before it disappeared down a bank by the pond and into the distance. "It was definitely a black cat," he said, "like a puma. It was far too big to be a dog and it was slinking across the field the way a large cat would. The tail was very long and thick, all the way to the end. That is what distinguished it. I wasn't scared, I was more shocked to see something like that. You don't expect to see a puma wandering in a local field. It didn't look like it was starved or anything - in fact it looked well-fed. My guess is that it has escaped from a zoo years ago and has been living wild on animals in the woods, or that someone abandoned it after the laws came out saying you couldn't keep wild cats as pets any more." Mr Hill spotted the wild cat at about 8am as he was starting work on the construction site. He called the police and they sent out an officer to check the area and examine paw prints Mr Hill thinks the cat may have left behind. I'll continue to update as and when I find anything. I'll go down at some point over the weekend and have a look around the site, but I hold little hope of any decent prints -

there's been a lot of torrential rain since the sighting.

Hampshire BBCRG representative Colin Lacey visited the area on the 3rd of July and reports:

I went down to the area of the sighting on Friday night, and had a look round. Apart from a large brown animal moving quickly through the woodland in the half-light a few yards ahead of me (turned out to be a roe deer, but enough to get the pulse racing!), there were no immediate signs.

I walked the perimeter of the pond twice, but was unable to see any footprints whatsoever in the clay, not even those of the police man or the photographer that snapped the image printed.

The pond lies in a narrow tapering clearing between three areas of woodland, leading through to open fields. The building site overlooks the pond only slightly, so you'd have to be in the right place on the site to see anything moving there.
I found a large footprint on the access track alongside the building site. Although the print looked roughly canine (German shepherd?) there didn't appear to be any claw marks. The ground was fairly hard though, due to being under trees and sheltered from the heavy rain. *(source: Colin Lacey)*

30th: Cheshire/England. Walking home from work, (approximately 7 miles East of Cheshire) as I do every night 5 times a week. I live next to corn fields and It is much quicker to walk down the dirt track. I have lived here for 17 years and have walked this route countless times. When I looked at my phone to see the time and then looked ahead and saw the back end of a large mottled grey animal disappear into the long grass. Now I see foxes all the time and occasionally the odd badger, pheasant, rabbit etc. But this was no ordinary animal the tail was about two and a half feet in length and poised in mid air as it stepped down into the long grass. it had defined back legs and was about three and a half foot in height. I was quite shocked at what I had seen and ran to the spot which was approximately forty feet ahead. To see if I could see the corn move. Because this in my opinion was definitely a wild big cat you here about, there is no doubt in my mind. The tail was more than a give away because looked approximately two or three inches thick and that's not normal! *(source: BCIB report form)*

30th: Essex/England. One mile outside of Ongar, a large black cat described as a panther was spotted crossing a country lane. *(source: BCIB report form)*

JULY

1st: Yorkshire/England. A big cat was spotted on Elland Road and reported to the West Stand security office of Leeds United football stadium. After spotting the creature in the Fullerton car park himself, security manager Jeff Stoyles said, "I thought it was a wind-up at first. I walked in to the car park and at first couldn't see a thing. Then I noticed something in the distance walking away. From where I was standing it looked like a very large domestic cat, but as I got closer it growled and leapt away to the far side of the car park. It frightened the life out of me!" (source: Leeds United press office – later turned out to be a hoax)

2nd: Co Cavan/Irish Republic. Gardía in Co. Cavan have been conducting patrolled searches outside the town after sightings of a large black cat. The cat, reported to be larger than a Labrador dog, was spotted running across a field and climbing up a tree in the Kilmore area, west of Cavan town. Similar sightings have been reported in Co. Monaghan in recent weeks, leading to speculation that an animal such as a puma might be at large. Cavan gardia said three callers had reported seeing the cat at around 10pm last night. There have been no further reported sightings since then. *(source: Charlie McGuinness)*

3rd: Hampshire/England. "I was walking along the banks of the River Arle at Arlesford in Hampshire when I spotted another large cat. It was stalking ducklings on the other side of the river for approx 20 minutes. It was no more than 35 feet away from me and I had a very clear sight of it. It was approx twice as large as a typical house cat with the most remarkable colouring and head shape. Seen straight on, the face and head were black with slight white markings under each eye. The ears seemed exceptionally large and pointy and were placed in an unusual position on the head - more to the side than I think usual in house cats. This gave the head an almost perfectly triangular shape. Very odd. It was short-haired and the trunk fur was mainly off-white with some bits of brown but not in spots nor stripes. The tail was entirely black as were the legs. It struck a pose that was akin to a hunting dog with one forepaw raised while it sniffed the air. It was sleek and muscular. It looked and moved both like a jungle cat and something not feline at all. In fact, when I first saw it, I though it might have been an otter. It didn't manage to get any ducks. Some locals told me that there had been an animal park/exotic zoo nearby. They thought it had closed or that many animals had escaped. They thought that what I'd seen might have been an escapee or a hybrid." *(source: BCIB report form)*

3rd: Greater London/England. Another large black cat has been spotted in the area. Described as bigger than an Alsatian. *(source: Andy Williams)*

4th: Devon/England. Kim Locke from Ringmore said, "I was driving home from work, and as I approached Seven Stones Corner near St Annes Chapel, a large black cat jumped out of the hedge onto the road in front of me. As I got closer to it I could see it was like a panther, and as I slowed down it stood and stared at me for about 30 seconds. It then jumped back in the hedge. I was more amazed then scared." *(source: Western Morning News)*

5th: Renfrewshire/Scotland. A large black cat spotted by the Knaps Dam. *(source: Mark Fraser)*

6th: Lincolnshire/England. A large black cat spotted near Hemingby. *(source: Mark Fraser)*

7th: Greater London/England. A large black cat has been spotted several times over the last few weeks in and around Stone, Gravesend, Meopham, New Ash Green, Cobham and Vigo Village, and nearby Bexley. Described as bigger than an Alsatian, the latest sighting brings the total to a dozen reports. *(source: News Shopper)*

circa 8th: Lancashire/England. Unconfirmed reports of a large cat hit by a car on the outskirts of Preston. *(source: Christopher Johnston)*

8th: Suffolk/England. On the 8th July whilst walking the dog in Dunwich forest I saw what I can only describe as a Lynx-like cat. My wife and I came to a "crossroads" in the forest and stopped to call the dog, which tends to disappear into the woods and do its own thing but answers the whistle very well. I called her back and whist looking around to see where she was; I spotted a movement to my right. When turning to face the movement I saw a large cat, light brown to tan in colour moving into the brush at the edge of the tree line I only saw it from the shoulders back. It was about 3ft 6ins along the shoulder line and the tail hung low to the floor and turned up at the end. It didn't hurry, just slowly moved out of site. Unfortunately my wife didn't see it and still doubts what I say I saw. The dog however did notice, because at the same time she appeared and took off through the same hole that the cat had used and started to bark as she does when spotting rabbits, but before she got too involved, if it was a cat, I whistled her to come back. She did but kept looking back as we walked on down the path. There were no signs on the ground because of the pine needles and of course where the dog had followed through. *(source: BCIB report form)*

10th: Gloucestershire/England. A dark cat, with an almost black back and head, also with black stripes down the outside of each leg was spotted on the outskirts of Catbrook Village at 14.30hrs. Further described as having ears and tail fairly typical of a domestic cat, about the size of a dog-fox but with long legs compared to its body length. The witness reports: "We were staying in the forest of Dean, on a 10 day camping Holiday, when my wife picked up a local walk leaflet. A circular walk from the Fountain inn public house, during that walk along a lane just before Catbrook the cat came from a track from our left into the lane about twenty five yards in front of us, heading the direction we where travelling, stopped looked around at us, then continued around the corner, all four of us saw it. And at once remarked, that was a big cat." *(source: BCIB report form)*

10th: Aberdeenshire/Scotland. At 10am on South Deeside Road, ½ mile from Brig of Feugh, a large black cat, about 4 times bigger than a domestic cat, walked out in front of a car and crossed the road into a driveway. *(source: Mark Fraser)*

11th: Cornwall/England. Sheep attacked on a smallholding in Cornwall. The owners believe it may have been the victim of a big cat. *(source: Mark Fraser)*

11th: Shropshire/England. A large ginger cat that had a tail with a white tip was spotted at around 22.00hrs near Ford, Shewsbury. Ears and tail were the shape of a domestic, the length of the cat was 75cm/height 50cm. Seen near to badger holes. Crouched by a tree for at least ten minutes for no apparent reason. When the witness moved it ran off into the nearest field. *(source: BCIB report form)*

11th: Devon/England. The witness reports: "I disturbed this cat when I went to the top of my Garden. The cat was in bushes, which back on to a railway line on the edge of Dartmoor. The cat moved from where it was lying, I saw the tail and length of the cat, it couldn't have been a domestic cat it was to large and I know all the cats in the neighbourhood. Then it disappeared into the undergrowth. This is the second time I have seen this cat. The cat was spotted at around 17.00hrs, jet-black with a very thick and long tail." The witness did not see the ears, as the cat was "hiding in the bushes." It had a "long body" and was about 2 ½ feet in height.

"The last time I saw it was again in Ivybridge near the rugby ground early one morning. I saw it walking down the middle of a country lane down the centre of the road. Which I thought was strange for a cat to walk down the middle of the road, but as it turned is head to one side its head was large when it noticed me it ran up the banking and ran through a field."

The BCIB resident zoological adviser Chris Moiser went round to see the gentleman, and reports: "I looked up this chap's telephone number in the local directory and went round to see him tonight, taking my puma cut out as a size reference. At the back of the house where the sighting took place there is an area of dense woody scrub, forming a strip of woodland followed by a cycle path and then the railway track, all appropriately fenced in. The gentleman concerned is a family man with several young children who presents himself as very rational and normal. He has a Collie type dog and identified the cat as being about the same size as a collie and/or my cut out. He glimpsed the animal for just a few seconds, before it turned and made its way back into the undergrowth. He would have been within 20 feet of it.

Examination of the area revealed dense undergrowth, apparently belonging to Railtrack or an associated company, fencing relatively well maintained and, although the area had been played in by children until a few years ago, it is not played in now - the few holes in the fence would make access unlikely because of the density of greenery there. The area is contiguous with the South Dartmoor border countryside with, at worst, the animal only having to cross the station car park to move from the moor border to this part of the town. There have been sightings in this area before by other witnesses.

The animal was sighted on Monday 11/07/05, at about 4.45 - 5.00pm, during a hot spell. It may be significant that this gentleman's garden had a pond, as do several others in the estate.

As we came back from looking at the site we met the neighbour's (medium large) male black domestic cat, which was said to be similar, except for size. Witness very credible." *(source: BCIB report form & Chris Moiser)*

15th: Kinross-shire/Scotland. A large black cat was spotted at 17.45hrs on the near the B9097 near Kinross. Eoin McDonald caught a glimpse of the rear of the cat as it went into undergrowth. The tail was about 2ft long, curved upwards and was covered in short hair. Eoin estimates the cat to be 18 inches to 2ft over the rear end in height. He said, "I caught a fleeting glimpse of what appeared to be a big cat as it went into undergrowth on the south side of the B9097 about 500 yards west of the Vane Farm RSPB centre. All I saw was the mid section backwards and the shape was distinctly feline. About three years ago I saw a similar sized animal about one mile east of this location." *(source: BCIB report form)*

15th July 2005: Lothians/Scotland. Maintenance manager John Doran, 47, believes he saw a puma at around 5pm on Friday in the grounds of Pittendreich Nursing Home in Lasswade where he works. He said, "I saw this thing in the grounds so I ran and got a pair of binoculars. It was massive with a long tail and pointed ears. I'm sure it was a puma." *(source: Edinburgh Evening News)*

15th: Mod/England. A sighting of a large black 'cat' on the base by two visitors. The time was around 22.28hrs; the witnesses were driving through the base when a large, 8ft black animal ran out across the road and disappeared into fields on the opposite side. I asked the witness to describe what he saw, but he was unable. The only description given was that of a "scooby doo dog" lookalike. *(source: Mark Fraser. Location undisclosed)*

18th: County Durham/England. A large black "panther" type cat was spotted near Tynedale by a family at Lowgate near the Rainbow Trust's Fernstone House two weeks ago. Shortly after, it was spotted by dog walker Marjorie Douglas at Duke's Wood, Hexham. She said it walked across the path in front of her, from one side of the wood to another. She adds, "I was walking the dog in the wood. A very large cat crossed in front of my path. It didn't stop at all. It had a very long body and was very dark in colour. It definitely wasn't a fox or a domestic cat or anything like that. It was a very unusual sight because you don't normally see something like that in the wood." *(source: Hexham Courant)*

18th: Dundee - Perth/Scotland. A large black cat seen crossing the dual carriageway on the A90 near Scone Palace. The witness said the animal was running at a "very fast pace" and jumped a hedge, disappearing into a field. He also describes the animal as "fabulous and elegant." *(source: Dundee Courier)*

20th: Yorkshire/England. A man had been driving home along the A614, not far from Pocklington, when a large mysterious creature stepped onto the road and crossed in front of his car. Kenneth Pinney, of Derby, had been travelling along the stretch of road between the Shiptonthorpe roundabout and Holme-on-Spalding Moor at about 6.30pm when the creature emerged from the roadside bushes.

"I was driving towards the M62 to get home," he said, "when it ran straight out in front of me, although I did manage to avoid it. It happened so quickly I never really thought about stopping. But it was so big that it looked to take up about half of the road on one side. It was not black, it looked more like a dark brown colour perhaps, and it was definitely not a dog." *(source: Pocklington Post)*

20th: Lothians/Scotland. Alistair Ross spotted what he believed was a big cat from his cottage window near Roslin. He thought straight away it was something unusual, although he had previously been sceptical about big cats in Scotland. He grabbed his camera and fired off a series of shots, one which is reproduced here with Mr Ross's permission.

Mr Ross, 54, who works as a bus driver, estimates the animal's body was about 3ft long with a tail measuring about 1½ft. He said, "I usually watch pheasants and other wildlife from my downstairs window all year. This area is a haven for wildlife. There was no way this was a domestic cat, its body was around 3ft long and jet black. I have never seen anything like it in my life." He added, "The animal was massive, you could see it prowling about the field. It sort of crept along, its whole body moving very slowly. I ran out of the house, picked up my camera and stood about 50 yards from the beast, hoping to get as close as possible without putting myself in danger." Mr Ross was able to watch the cat prowling back and forth for about 15 minutes before it finally disappeared from view. His Gourlaw Cottages home is about half a mile from Roslin on the Penicuik road. *(source: Alistair Ross & Edinburgh Evening News)*

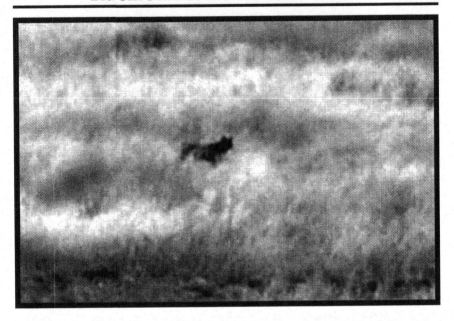

Big Cat sighted in Lothians, Scotland (Picture courtesy of Alistair Ross)

23rd: Surrey/England. Crookham Village: "I was driving along the A287 towards Farnham in Surrey, I noticed an odd looking animal walking across a field between 25m and 50m away.

I drive for about four hours a day on country roads, and am used to seeing foxes and the like, and this was not a dog-like animal. It did not seem to be walking with the wolf-like gait of a dog or fox.

After getting over the shock, I turned in to the next lane (going off towards Crookham Village) and parked. There was no sign of the animal, but in the same field I found a long (8 inches) clump of droppings (actually it looked like a cat's fur ball). The object was flaky and filled with inch long, brown coarse hair - perhaps rabbit hair. I collected some of this with gloves the next day - which I now have in a sealed bag in my fridge."

The witness further describes the cat as "mid-light brown, with no visible markings, with a flat muzzle and relatively small head. I didn't really notice the ears. The real give away was the tail: almost as long as the body, thin and muscular, and not at all bushy. Perhaps the size of a sheep, with a tail almost as long as the body. *(source: BCIB report form)*

25th July 2005: Cumbria/England. A large black cat was spotted in Furness and a pedigree sheep that was ripped to pieces is thought to have been killed by this mysterious feline. Retired teacher Eliza Hall, 57, saw the beast from her home in Scales, near Ulverston. Three days later, Ian Rawlinson, of Quarry Bank Farm, Marton, found one of his pedigree Suffolk Gimmer sheep savaged. Mrs Hall, the district commissioner for the High Furness and Duddon Scout Association, said, "I was just getting ready to go out when I looked out of my bedroom window over the garden and saw a big black cat at the back of our house. It was like a panther - long and thin - and no way could it have been a dog or anything like that. It was definitely a big black cat."

The attack on Mr Rawlinson's sheep happened at Bennett Bank, near Roanhead, Barrow. *(source: Hexham Courant)*

25th: Ayrshire/Scotland. Passengers travelling on the Kilmarnock to Glasgow route say they grabbed a fleeting glimpse of the animal minutes after leaving Dunlop Station, early in the morning. John Dewar, a reporter for the Ayrshire Extra told Mark Fraser that the cat looked "mangy", was brown in colour and sat on a fallen log, sunning itself. The witness, George Braidwood, said, "I was just chatting to my friend and looking out of the window. Suddenly I saw this big cat on top of a rotting tree and pointed out to the others on the train. I was very excited. Four people sitting behind us saw it too. It was only in view for a matter of seconds but long enough for me to get a good look. It was brown with a long tail and appeared pretty thin and mangy but too big to be a dog or fox – it was a puma or lynx." *(source: John Dewar of the Ayrshire Extra)*

26th: Gloucestershire/England. Bob Austin reported seeing a large jet-black "panther" to the *Wilts & Gloucestershire Standard* near his Stratton home. Mr Austin, who is a chief executive for the Cotswold District Council, said, "I am absolutely certain about what I saw. It was about the size of a Labrador but definitely not a domestic cat or dog. It was about 75 yards away and this cat-like animal was right on the corner of Grange Court and the open play area. It was standing absolutely still with an arched back and for a moment I thought it might have been a prank, but then it dropped its back, turned in a circle and walked towards the primary school. I didn't follow it because it was bigger the my dog and thought it wouldn't be a good idea - it was about two feet high and four feet long, with a thick tail." (source: *Wilts & Gloucestrshire Standard*)

27th: Carmarthenshire/Wales. Vague Reports of a puma spotted walking through a field. *(source: unknown)*

30th: Dartmoor/England. The Sunday Independent reports on nervous residents around the village of East Ogwell in Devon. One witness reports that the large cat "looked powerful, with strong shoulder blades." But Mike Healy, owner of a four-year-old, two stone pet cat (pictured above) explained, "That just had to be Sebastian. The fields where the 'panther' was seen are his hunting grounds. "He slinks around as if he's John Wayne but he's just a big softie." *(source: Sunday Independant)*

31st: East Yorkshire/England. I think my wife and I may have seen the elusive big cat that is said to be living in the East Riding of Yorkshire in the Holderness area. We were out for an early evening drive on Sunday 31st July in the Sunk Island area (nearest village is Ottringham) and spotted a beast, which caught both our attentions because of its apparent size and shape. *(source: BCIB report form)*

AUGUST

2nd: Euxton Lancashire/England. Leyland man, and his wife (name withheld) were driving along Runshaw Lane, going to the Plough pub for a late meal at 8.30 pm when they saw a cat like animal stroll across the road and disappear into the undergrowth on the far side. It was described as "a sort of light-brown in colour", with a head which was small for its body, and a "stub-nose" like a wild cat. The witness consulted the internet and thought the animal was "like an ocelot or lynx, only smaller." *(source: BCIB report form)*

Early August 2005. A ten foot long wicker sculpture of the "Beast of Blackdown" was stolen and subsequently found abandoned. *(Western Morning News*

Early August 2005: Dorset/England. A panther-like creature was seen by six members of the public at the Golden Cap caravan park, near Chideock. It was seen in a thicket about 200 yards from the beach. The creature was black, had a cat-like face and long tail. *(Source: Dorset Echo)*

3rd: Derbyshire/England. Colin Prime, a senior account manager at Linings and Hoses Ltd. on the Airfield Industrial Estate, was driving along the north by-pass road from the A515 to the A52 at 0900hrs when a large "dirty brown cat with a long tail" ran out across the road. He said, "It was about 5ft long, its body was not built like a lion but more like a lynx or a cheetah." It headed towards Ashbourne golf club. *(Ashbourne News Telegraph)*

7th: Devon/England. Via Chris Moiser, report regarding a non-native cat sighting.

"Following information received from a local reporter I telephoned Mrs. Vicky Staplehurst and subsequently met her in the entrance to a local smallholding near Loddiswell in South Devon at 4.00pm on Monday 8th August 2005. Whilst waiting there I spoke to the smallholding owner (Mrs. Staplehurst had alerted him to us meeting there and obtained his permission); he was interested and was aware of many other cat sightings in the area. He had apparently had a report of a large cat seen climbing his fence in the recent past. He was aware of people in the area having sighted cats and not having reported them for fear of ridicule.

When Mrs. Staplehurst arrived she too was aware of other people having witnessed cat sightings in the locality - but this was the first one that she had seen. She took me approximately 100 yards back up the road towards California Cross (this road is the unclassified road, a left turn off the road that passes the California Cross pub and garage - the turn is just South of these landmarks and is signposted Loddiswell and Kingsbridge). The sighting had been made at 8.45pm the previous night. It was of a black cat - the size of a Great Dane she had initially stated. The animal had entered a field through an open gate.

On attending the site with her and a plywood cut out of a cat silhouette, (medium puma or small black leopard size) pictured below, she confirmed her position in the road - she had been driving a saloon car - and that this was the

field entrance. The field sloped up from the road and then fell away into a large valley with deciduous woodland going up the slope on the other side before giving way to open scrub. To the North was the Blackdown Rings ancient monument site. The field was a large one with a cereal crop planted, and the crop appeared to be about ready to harvest at 45 - 60 cm high. There was a possible animal track through it to the left of the entrance gate, along the side of the gate.

Mrs. Staplehurst reviewed her estimated size of the animal when looking at the cut-out, and said that a Great Dane would be too tall - she thought that the animal that she saw was the size of the cut out. The Great Dane size was explained because she had tried to mention something bigger than a collie, and a Great Dane was all she could think of quickly. She also told me of a farm across the valley where dogs were kept in kennels outside and used for hunting. They had been making a lot of noise at night recently - this was unusual behaviour on their part.

Mrs. Staplehurst presented herself as a sensible lady who was pleased to have seen what she did, and who was disappointed that her friend, who had wanted to see such an animal had not been with her at the time. She had not been able to stop and watch the animal because of other traffic on the road.

This area is contiguous with the reported positions of many other sightings of large black cats, such as the giant black cat seen at St Anne's Chapel reported in the Western Morning News earlier this month"
This case was subsequently reported in Ivybridge Gazette 26/08/2005. *(Source: Chris M. Moiser)*

8th: Cheshire/England. At about 9.45 last night, myself and my brother were fishing at Castlefields reservoir in Runcorn. We were walking round the reservoir and we saw a black feline about the size of a Labrador (my brother thought it was a Lab at first). It moved in an unmistakably catlike manner, and we saw it from approximately 10 feet away, as it leapt across our path and disappeared into the undergrowth, it was clear conditions, though starting to become dusk. We only saw it for 3-5 seconds.

I am thoroughly convinced it was clearly a cat (I grew up in Africa and have seen many wild cats from leopard, cheetah, civet, wild cat, genet, caracal on many occasions, and so feel I can accurately tell the difference between domestic dog and a non-indigenous species of large cat!) *(Source: BCIB report form)*

circa 9th: Yorkshire/England. I had two clear days so I took off. I packed my bike and tent and headed for the North Yorkshire Moors. The weather was kind, and I did 60 miles walking, running and riding. For those that know the moors, I was following the route of The Lyke Wake walk, which runs between Osmotherly and Ravenscar. I was on the stretch running eastwards towards the road that runs down to Hutton le Hole. It was about 6.30pm. As I started up a steep slope,

I was aware of something moving fast from left to right about 200 hundred yards ahead of me. At first I thought it was a large dog. It wasn't. It was a large cat, about the size of a sheep. Black, or very dark brown. I reached for my camera, but by the time I had pulled it out of my bag, the animal was over the hills and far away.

I reported the sighting and was told that this was the first sighting of a cat in that area. After the cat had gone I climbed on my bike. I think I may have set a new world speed record for that stretch of the moors .*(Source: The Champion, South-port)*

10th: Hertfordshire/England. "I wonder if you could give me some advice. My friend, who lives near Kings Langley in Hertfordshire phoned last night. That morning she had found her daughters pony in one of their fields with puncture marks around one of its ankles and also several large scratches from the top of the leg down almost to the bottom. She said that it looks as if the animals leg has been chewed on its stifle. By the sound if it, no other animal other than a big cat could have inflicted these injuries, not even a brave fox. I am pretty sure that a badger would not attack a pony.

I have read on the internet that there was a sighting of a big cat sometime ago in this area, indeed, last year a mare belonging to a friend of hers had 2 puncture marks in it's belly, approximately 3 inches apart, but there was no other injury and so it is possible that it caught itself on something in the field.

Is it your opinion that an electric fence around the field perimeter would keep a big cat away? Advice greatly appreciated. On further speaking with my friend further there appear to have been other sightings in the area. The wound on her pony is not healing well as it is very deep. Her vet would not attribute the wound to anything but did discount a fox, I have looked on the internet but been unable to find any evidence of badger attacks on livestock or humans. There are wildboars there but the claw marks on the pony are not consistent with attack by a wild boar. The vet did also say that there had been other injuries in the area which were 'inexplicable'." *(Source: Nigel Spencer)*

11th: Derbyshire/England A tourist spotted a mysterious large cat at the Pikehorse Farm Caravan Park, Thorpe Cloud, run by Bill Gallimore. The witnesses were just leaving the park when they saw it jumping around rocks. They had binoculars and got quite a good view of the animal, apparently. *(Source: Asbourne News & Telegraph)*

12th: Caernarfonshire, Gwynedd/Wales. "I am pretty sure I saw a big cat cross my path about 10 a.m. on Friday 12th August. I was out running around the bottom of the North side of a mountain called Garn Fadryn, near Llaniestyn in North Wales. It is pretty remote and there are only a couple of farmhouses nearby situated off a rough track. About 120 yards ahead of me, on the track, a fawny coloured animal about the size of a medium sized dog, with a small head and long thin tail, held horizontally to the body, trotted across the track, glanced briefly at me and then disappeared into the bracken to my right.

I was pretty stunned and tried to convince myself it had been a very large fox or something, but the coat wasn't red enough, it moved like a cat, not a dog, the tail was too long and not bushy and it was far too big. I turned on my heels and ran back the way I'd come feeling very uneasy.

I'm not prone to imagining that I've seen strange beasts or aliens or anything like that, but am pretty convinced that what I saw was a very large cat. A local man told me that a farmer a few miles away has claimed to have seen something similar." *(Source: BCIB report form)*

circa 12th: Ayrshire/Scotland. Witness, while out walking her Airdales near the ICI Nobel plant in Stevenston, has noticed strange behaviour from her dogs on two occasions.

The first time her dog was away chasing rabbits. He started to bark in what she calls 'fierce guard barking', which he doesn't do when chasing prey. He returned trembling and with his tail between his legs; not a reaction to humans, whom he would normally ignore.

Six months later she was out and the dogs had run on ahead. She saw what she thought was a large black dog with her young bitch in pursuit. At first she assumed it was her other 'dale, but suddenly realised that he was a bit behind. The bitch suddenly stopped, dropped her tail and started to tremble. The dog was ok, having appeared not to have seen the animal, but her bitch didn't recover her "happy tail" until they were at least a quarter of a mile away from the scent that she had picked up.

She knows that it wasn't a deer or another dog as they would have continued the chase but has no idea what could be that large that would have frightened both dogs. *(Source: Kaz BCIB research group)*

13th: Yorkshire/England. A large black cat spotted between Great Ayton and Guisborough at Pinchinthorpe in North Yorkshire. The witness reports: "Whilst being driven home by my mother on the A173 between Great Ayton and Guisborough at Pinchinthorpe at about 1-o-clock in the morning, a large animal leaped out in front of the car from the nearside. The headlights were on full beam, and if we had been travelling any quicker we would probably have collided with it. The animal was most definitely a large black cat but with a bushy, feathery tail and a furry body. My initial impression was that of an Afghan hound, but its movements were distinctly feline and it had leapt from the side of the road to the other side of the white line in one bound. We did not actually see the animal take off and were only aware of it as its body passed through the headlights.

We did not get a clear view of head but it had a long tail - about 3ft long and bushy in appearance. The length of the animal was about 3ft in height and 4ft long not including the tail." *(Source: BCIB report form)*

14th: Dorset/England. A scaffolding company worker reported defending himself with a large piece of wood after sighting a black panther at an industrial estate near Bournemouth International Airport. *(Source: BBC News)*

14th: Derbyshire/England. An Ashbourne couple watched a "jaguar-sized, black cat" kill and drag a hare into nearby bushes. This occurred at Dovedale in the Peak District, and the couple were walking along the Dove at 8.15pm when they saw the beast kill the hare on the hillside. They alerted a nearby fisherman and the three of them watched the cat carry its supper into what appeared to be a series of holes below bushes.

The man told the News Telegraph: "It was about three times the size of a normal cat, like a jaguar, and it was jet black with a long tail. It carried the hare off like a leopard would drag an antelope." *(Source: News Telegraph)*

15th: Devon/England. "I received an email earlier today that was sent by a lady in Loddiswell. She has asked that I keep her name and address confidential in view of previous publicity, and the worry of attracting people with guns. She has consented to being identified as being at "a smallholding near Loddiswell". Anyway the data is follows:

Between 9.00pm last night and 7.00 am this morning a sheep was killed in her small flock. The sheep are a small variety of breeds and this was a male, between 4 - 6 months of age. The body was covered, but left where it was found until I got there (before lunchtime).

I found the animal to be a well nourished male, the size was consistent with the breed and stated age at death. The body was in good condition, but with the head missing and the neck being severed at the cervical vertebrae 3-4 area. One vertebrae was actually broken through. The soft tissues were cut in a way that was consistent with sharp teeth, but not a sharp knife, machete or axe. The limbs were easily flexed and there was no evidence of rigor mortis present, except possibly (slightly) in the back legs. In view of the overnight temperature and the time at which the body was found, I would say that death occurred nearer the 7.00am time in the available time envelope, rather than the night before. There were no discernable claw marks anywhere on the body. The wool was dense though, and claws may have engaged to hold the animal without penetrating the skin.

Subsequent discussion with the lady's husband revealed that when he was called to look at the animal the rest of the flock were still very frightened, and that there had been something of a commotion in the far end of the paddock when several rabbits suddenly burst out of cover and ran towards the couple and deceased sheep. At this time the couple's dogs were still in the house. These dogs are medium sized, of a breed regularly seen in the countryside, but not noted for ferocity. They apparently frequently refuse to go out at night.

The lady did see a large black cat sometime about 1990/91, which she discussed with Nigel Brierly at the time. Her husband heard a growl from some bushes nearby two years ago. Additionally the couple had received a report of a local tradesman having seen a cat (large and black) clear the front gate of the property, run across the road and jump into/through the hedge on the far side.

Examination of the paddock was difficult due to the high stands of nettles involved and the cover contained within it. There was a fairly efficient fence running around the entire circumference of it, in places the sheep wire was secondary to an original Devon bank/wall structure. No badger tracks were found entering or leaving the field. The conditions underfoot were dry due to recent weather, and in places regularly disturbed by sheep hooves. No footprints other than those of the sheep and humans were found, except at the small pond which showed evidence of several birds drinking there regularly.

This sheep killing is within one half mile of the Vicky Staplehurst sighting. The body does present a confusing picture though; it was clearly not killed by a fox or a dog. A fully grown puma or leopard could have carried the body away for later consumption. A badger could have removed the head, producing the neck trauma seen, but would probably have attacked the body first and, if given the chance would have almost certainly opened the abdomen Similarly, I would have expected a badger to have produced some trauma to the sheep's legs, rather than just going straight for the neck.

On reflection I believe that this sheep was killed either by an unidentified big cat which was disturbed, or by a badger that was similarly disturbed. In either case the head was removed from the field.

This is the first sheep that these people have lost, and it was a small sheep." *(Source: Chris M Moiser)*

circa 15th : Essendon/England. Jeff Leo was hunting rabbits at dusk with his 4 Lurcher dogs near Hatfield London Country Club, when a large black cat pelted out of the undergrowth. Interestingly he had seen a similar (or the same) cat, almost a year before in almost exactly the same place. He described it as a lot bigger than a normal cat and with a very long thick tail. *(Source: Welwyn & Hatfield Times)*

15th: Lancashire/England. A large tabby coloured cat spotted near Bleasdale, around the size of a Labrador. The witness reports: "A farmer next door to my friend saw big cat. Spoke to other farmers in area who have seen it too. We saw what we think was a puma two years ago at rivers edge at Dunsop Bridge. Was told someone released three big cats near Dunsop in 1996.

We know of definite release of large amount of big cats in late 70's at Alston near Longridge. Lately, big cats have been seen around periphery of Chipping." *(Source: Chris Johnston)*

15th: Hertfordshire/England. Welham Green resident Joanne Cetti came face to face with the 'Beast of Brookmans Park' as she walked her dog on Bradmore Lane at 6am. Joanne said, "I was walking along and saw this animal crossing the road about 200ft away. As it passed it definitely looked at me and then moved quicker. But I wasn't scared. I lived in Africa for three years and I've seen quite a lot of them.

I saw it very clearly - it's pretty much open country. I do see a lot of animals but this wasn't like anything else I've seen around here.

It was bigger, sleeker and moved completely differently. It was also very dark, like a panther." *(Source: Welwyn & Hatfield Times)*

circa 18th: Dorset/England. "On this particular night I couldn't sleep, so as it was a particularly brilliant night for stars here in West Bay, I thought I'd walk up the cliff path a bit to get away from the light pollution and do a bit of stargazing.

I found a nice bench, laid down - perfect, pitch black, loads of stars. Very relaxing until a few minutes later, something large and dog-sized galloped at speed right up to the bench! I sat up with a start, and the animal then shot off in another direction. It was then that I remembered my father's stories of seeing the 'beast of Dorset' several times, and then I realized that maybe sitting alone in the pitch black in the Dorset countryside for the sake of astronomy maybe wasn't one of my better ideas. I did not see the animal unfortunately." *(Source: Merrily Harpur)*

20th: Dorset/England. PC John Snellin of the Dorset police warned people not to go near any large cats sighted. He also explained that the Dorset Constabulary have actually drawn up contingency plans if a large cat should appear. He said a woman who works in the control room at Dorset Police had reported hearing a "growling noise" from inside bushes on Canford Heath in Poole, as she walked with her mother on 20 August at 20.00hrs. PC Snellin added: "A loud roar like a big cat came from the bushes. They decided to run for it and as they ran off they heard another roar. She was a bit shook up." *(Source: Dorset Echo)*

20th: Banffshire/Scotland. Witness spotted a three feet long and two feet high black cat with rounded ears on the outskirts of Tomintoul. He reported: "I was at a T junction about to turn left towards Tomintoul. I looked right to see if there was any traffic and I saw a huge

black cat crossing the road slowly, on my right. This is the second time I have seen such an animal. About two years ago four of us disturbed a similar cat on a hill near Aboyne." *(Source: BCIB report form)*

circa 21st: Dorset/England. Police in Dorset urged the public to ring 999 should they spot a big cat. The warning came after Wiltshire salesman Kevin Hamersley claimed he saw a puma in West Cliff Road, Bournemouth. Mr Hamersley saw what he said was a puma prowling near his hotel. He was walking back to his room with a couple of friends when the incident happened. He claims the cat was 2ft tall, and standing in the middle of the road. The time was 04.30hrs. He said, "It was as big as a dog, but it wasn't a dog. It stopped in the middle of the road and looked at us for about two or three minutes. We were just trying to work out what it was and it just stood there frozen, looking at us, before it turned around and ran off. I thought it might be a puma. I watch a lot of wildlife programmes so I know my big cats. I don't think they would attack humans unless you provoked them, but they are meat eaters so I didn't hang around. I didn't want to get gashed by its big claws. I'm now convinced there's either a puma or a lynx on the loose in Bournemouth." *(Source: Merrily Harpur)*

22nd: Fife/Scotland. Reports of a large black cat spotted in a garden in Anstruther, Fife. The cat was about 20 yards from the witness and was about 3ft in length. *(Source: The Scotsman)*

23rd: Northamptonshire/England. A panther-like creature was seen by Michelle Deakin as she was travelling between Collingtree and Milton Malsor. She believes the animal she spotted lurking by the roadside was in fact a puma, after doing some research on the Internet. At first the 32-year-old housewife, who lives in Bugbrooke, initially thought that it was a dog. "The animal moved like a large dog," she said, "but when we got closer we realised that it was some sort of cat," she explained. It was black and also slightly grey in colour and had a very muscular build. The animal moved sleekly across the road and I also noticed that it had black rings around its tail. It was quite a shock to see something like that in the Northamptonshire countryside." *(Source: Northampton Chronicle & Echo 26/8/05)*

23rd: Kent/England. Large black cat seen at Barming/Tovil at 19.10hrs. Described as being 2 - 3ft in height, and 3-4ft long. The witness watched it walk down a tractor track in a field heading towards a wooded area. *(Source: BCIB report form)*

24th: Hampshire/England. "I was walking my dog (Newfoundland) down

"Dark Lane", Hinton, Hants, on Tues evening around dusk and I'm convinced an ABC was in the field beside us. There were growls and rustlings coming from a field of maize. Now a big cat has to be pretty brave to take on a big dog like that - he weighs about 50 kilos - so we calmly (?) walked back to the car and drove off, though the hairs on the back of my neck were standing on end at that time.

There's very definitely "something" in this area, and has been for about two or three years. Anyone of you experts care to examine the scenes for pug marks, if nothing but to put my mind at rest? I admit - brave man that I am (not!)- I'm too scared to examine these areas myself.

Makes me wonder though, especially the reports about ABCs in Bournemouth town centre, this area borders the New Forest, so if there are cats about, why do they come in so close to "man territory" with so much natural food for them in the wild places? *(Source: BCIB report form)*

28th: Hertfordshire/England. I thought you might like to know that at about 11.00 am today, I am sure I saw a big black cat like a puma very near to Knebworth house in Hertfordshire. I was in my car on the A1 when I looked to my left and there, across a field in front of a wood, was a puma-like cat walking.
It was about 2ft high at the shoulders with a thick long tail held out in a horizontal position. I was quite amazed that it didn't seem to be very afraid of being seen. *(Source: Nigel Spencer)*

28th: Ayrshire/Scotland. "At 12.45am on Sunday 28th August I saw what only could be described as a very large black cat. I was taking the turn off from the A77 toward Kilmarnock just past the Fenwick hotel." *(Source: Mark Fraser)*

circa 29th: Derbyshire/England. Police found large footprints which belongs to an "as yet[...]unidentified animal" around the remains of sheep kills. Several sheep have been killed in recent weeks around the Denby and Kilburn areas.

Cllr John Grace, who represents the wards of Denby and Kilburn, owns ten acres of land between Derby Road and Station Road, Denby. He has been forced to sell his lambs after five of them were picked off in a matter of weeks. A fully grown ewe was also killed and eaten in one attack. Cllr Grace said, "There is hardly anything left of them - just a spine and skull with no flesh whatsoever. The legs and skin are completely gone. I don't know what can have done it, but there was wool everywhere. I don't think it can be people who are responsible. I'm worried about bringing my children down here because you just don't know." *(Source: Derbyshire Today)*

SEPTEMBER

1st: Norfolk/England. Bressingham resident Martin Ayre reported seeing a large black cat-like creature in his back garden. *(source: Diss Express)*

1st: MOD England. A large grey coloured cat spotted. *(Mark Fraser location undisclosed)*

2nd: Gloucestershire/England. Mac Gwinnett, who lives on the outskirts of Cirencester was just leaving his back garden when he spotted a large black cat. He said, "I opened the gate and stepped outside and saw this big cat. From where I was it looked as though it must have been 4ft long at least. I was about 200 yards away. It turned around and looked at me because I'd made a noise, then it plodded off into the bushes and trees." *(Source: Cirencester News)*

circa 2nd: Gloucestershire/England. CCTV footage came to light of what is believed by some to be a big cat walking across a zebra crossing in Cirencester. The footage came from security cameras situated in the centre of the town. The animal is shown walking over across the triangular sections which are 4.5ft in width. *The Wilts & Gloucestershire Standard* believes the cat appears to be as long, if not longer than those sections. The cat then walks away into nearby bushes. After the story of the footage appeared in local newspapers, another Cirencester resident came forward to say that he found over 20 prints in his garden last year. He said, "I think it tried to come in through the cat flap because our cat and dog were absolutely spooked. The following morning we noticed the footprints - there was loads of fresh soil around and you could see where he had come down from the woods. It's a genuine print, no doubt about it. But what it is I don't know - I was told to photograph it with something to compare its size. Some of the prints weren't as good but we photographed the best one we had." *(source: Wilts & Gloucestershire Standard & Cirencester News)*

2nd: Essex/England. The 'Beast of Ongar' has been spotted again, this time by two boys (ages unknown). Adam Taylor and Scott Prior saw the animal on Shelley Common. Adam's mother Belinda, told the *Guardian* Newspaper: "It was a big black cat, bigger than a Labrador and it was seen going into the hedge. At first Adam thought it was a fox but Scott said it wasn't because it was black."
Mrs Taylor now believes a big cat could have been responsible for scratches on her horse. "I just thought the other horses were bullying him," she said, "and

---

145

had pushed him into barbed wire, but thinking about it, it's too high up. He's had deep superficial scratches on one of his legs and round the quarter area near his tail."

Mrs Taylor, whose son's rabbits have been killed, has also been told of a deer that was found ripped apart in a ditch "with lumps of flesh all over the place". *(source: The Guardian)*

2nd: Dundee/Scotland. Lady saw a large black cat in a field East of Dundee, the animal was around 200 yards away. She describes it as 4-5ft in length and about 2ft in height. A week earlier her husband saw the cat in the same field. *(source: BCIB)*

3rd: Nottinghamshire/England. Anglers reported spotting a lynx near Peacock Close in Guthorpe. One said, "I heard a rustling in the grass and thought it was a fox. It was just starting to get dark, but I could clearly see the cat looking at me from the branch of a pear tree." *(Source: This is Nottingham)*

4th: Borders/Scotland. "I was driving from Roberton (village) to Hawick on B711. My wife exclaimed, "Look at that!" I slowed the car and we both watched this animal - larger than a fox, and certainly with a cat-like run for 10 - 15 seconds. I stopped car in the middle of the road and we both watched it slow down and move behind a dyke, about 100 yards away across the Borthwick Water. I went for my camera phone. My wife had been watching the beast behind the dyke, when a woman on a quad drove past on the river-side of the dyke with a greyhound (!) and an old lab. My wife did not see the beast again. We could NOT have mistaken either greyhound or old lab for the animal we saw - the colourings were much too dissimilar. We waited a while, but saw nothing of the animal again. Both my wife and I are convinced that it was not a fox, or dog".

The cat is described as being orange in colour with ears laid back, although unable to tell the shape and the overall size of the animal further than "larger than a full-grown fox". *(Source: Mark Fraser)*

4th: Norfolk/England. Motorist Bob Jennings contacted the Diss Express and reported that he and his wife had been travelling through Bressingham when they saw a large, dark-coloured animal cross the A1066 road. He said, "It was dark and we only saw it in the car headlights for a few seconds, but it looked like a big cat maybe the size of a German shepherd but with a longer body and tail," said Mr Jennings. *(source: Diss Express)*

5th: County Durham/England. I was walking in Durham Dales above Eastgate. I sighted a huge black cat about 200 yards away, near the quarry. It ran off into some woods so I wasn't able to get a photo. *(Source: Mark Fraser)*

6th: Somerset/England. At 15.00hrs, M. spotted what he is quite adamant was a lioness whilst driving along the M5. He reports: "I was driving South on the M5 in a van which was high enough for me to see into the fields, on my left I noticed a lioness or something very similar running across the field towards some sheep but I was doing about 65 m.p.h and didn't have a phone on me. I saw the cat for at least 15 seconds and got very excited but didn't want to stop as when it had actually sunk in what I had just saw I had probably travelled too far as I was on the motorway and couldn't stop or reverse.

The weather was fine and sunny and I thought nobody would take me seriously as my own family laughed, I was about 3 miles north travelling South of the welcome to Somerset sign." *(source: BCIB report form)*

6th: Fife/Scotland. A woman from Tanshall reported seeing a large black cat near Gilvenbank Park during the afternoon, which she promptly reported to the police. Susan McNab said, "I was on the other side of the road when I saw it coming down a small track - I was about 100 yards away from it. When I first saw it I thought it was a dog looking for its owner. It stood looking about and just watched me, watching it. Then it disappeared back into the bushes where it came from. It was a big jet-black cat which looked about the size of a border collie - I have my own dog-walking business so I know what a dog looks like and it definitely wasn't one. This is the first time I've seen a big cat, although I have read the stories about it. I wasn't scared because it was very peaceful, just minding it's own business. But it won't stop me from going into that area as I walk dogs there on a daily basis." *(source: Fife Free Press)*

circa 6th: Hertfordshire/England. Two teenage motorists had to brake sharply to avoid hitting a large mysterious feline on the A1000 near Herts Country Club, WGC. Passenger Ian Allen said, "We were driving down the road and all we saw was a pair of bright yellow eyes. At first we thought it was a dog or even a wolf but when we saw it properly it was a massive black thing with yellow eyes like a cat's. I've never seen anything like it."

Jamie Banham, who was driving, slammed on the brakes and beeped the horn which made the animal run into the undergrowth. Ian continues, "We didn't get out just in case. We weren't going outside with that out there! When we told everyone, they didn't believe us but we know what we've seen. It's like seeing a UFO." *(source Welwyn & Hatfield Times)*

Exact date not known: Dundee/Scotland. A lady was awoken early one morning by a very loud screaming noise coming from the old railway line at the foot of her garden. Several of her neighbours heard it also and believe it came from a big cat. *(source: BCIB)*

7th: Renfrewshire/Scotland. A large black cat spotted on the outskirts of Bishopton.

circa 7th: Hertfordshire/England. Scratch marks on a tree are said to be left by a big cat, according to Terry Moore, of The Cat Survival Trust. He reports in the Welwyn & Hatfield Times that he believes there is a black panther in Welwyn and a puma in Sacombe near Ware. He pointed out the scratch marks saying that these were the animals calling cards. He said, "It tends to come when the cats call. Their voices really carry and the pheromones travel for miles. There's absolutely no doubt in my mind, I am 110 per cent sure it is a black leopard." *(source: Welwyn & Hatfield Times)*.

7th: Staffordshire/England. Roger Cannon and his wife, who come from Hulme End, were returning from a shopping trip in Leek when they saw a large black cat near Warslow. Mr Cannon reported: "We decided to take the country road home so we went by The Mermaid pub across to Warslow by Eleven Lane Ends. Midway across the road I clearly saw an animal. It was jet black with a long flowing tail. It was much bigger than a cat, but nowhere as big as other sightings. It was the size of a possible cub. I now wonder if the stories of the panther in the Moorlands are true and they are breeding. We were about 60 yards from the animal. When it heard the car it just disappeared. I had no time to get out the camera. You first think it is a cat, but the size and the fact there are no houses in the area makes me think it is a cub." *(source: The Sentinel)*

9th: Dundee/Scotland. Sarah Higgings saw a large black cat near the BP garage on The Kingsway. *(Source: Dundee Courier)*

circa 9th: Hertfordshire/England. New footage, which hasn't been shown, is alleged to have been taken at an undisclosed location. A cat was spotted walking around a car park by a security company. One witness said it looked like a lion and was brown or sandy in colour. *(source: Hertfordshire Mercury)*

10th: Nottinghamshire/England. Anglers believe that there are two big cats living around Gunthorpe, one believed to be a lynx. They said they are living on wasteland at the back of Peacock Close. Carl Gibbs, who owns Peacock Lake, said he seen them on several occasions, and adds, "I met it on the path one night and, believe me, it was big. It had dark patches on its fur. It came through the fence from the field next door and stood looking at me before calmly walking away. On another occasion I surprised it in the next door neighbour's garden and it leapt over the fence in one bound. My father has seen it several times. I think it must live on rabbits. It is like a jungle at the back of the fields. You would never find it in there". *(Source: This is Nottingham)*

10th: Derbyshire/England. A local Ashbourne couple saw a large, black cat-like creature foraging in fields behind houses along Manor Road at around 08.30hrs. They said it was too big to be a domestic cat and was definitely not a dog, although similar in size to one. What breed it doesn't say. The woman said, "It had a long, thin tail. I called my husband over and said `what's that?' He got his binoculars out and had a better look. It was there for about five to 10 minutes." They thought it was too far away to get a photograph.

11th: Essex/England. Eight year old Connor Stockbridge of The Stree in Shearing was out with his mother, Suzette, and their dog Tara along a lane that bordered fields. Connor was riding ahead of his mother at around 19.00hrs. Suzette Stockbridge said, "I suddenly heard him scream and he shouted 'Mummy, Mummy'. I wondered what was going on and then I saw him coming back towards me on his bike and he was saying 'get Tara'. He was crying his eyes out and said 'I've seen a panther, a big black panther'. He said it was about the size of his bike with two big yellow fangs and it just leapt into the bushes after he saw it." She immediately came home as Connor was terrified but her other son, 13 year old Rhys, ran out with a camera to try and snap the animal but failed. Now Connor is too frightened to go anywhere near the area. *(Source: Herts & Essex Observer).*

Several dates: Hampshire/England. Five turkeys and two geese have been killed by what is believed to be a big cat. Carol Tennick, who keeps poultry and sheep at a stable yard in Broad Road, Monxton, reported that she did not believe it was the work of foxes because of the way the birds had been killed, and a fang mark that was left on the side of one of the carcasses. She said, "I have been ringing up zoos and the way the birds have been killed is not normal fox behaviour." *(source: Andover Advertiser)*

15th: Gloucestershire/England. "I live in Stanton Wick near Pensford, Bristol. My boyfriend has seen a big black cat. His son has seen the cat twice, on one occasion he was followed by the cat although he did not actually see it. His second sighting was a lot clearer and it appeared not to be phased by humans. Ben got a very good look at it and noticed the big green eyes. We live in the Winding House on the old Pensford Colliery, and the back of the house is surrounded by 27 acres of woodland and overgrowth. We are also surrounded by countryside

Yesterday around 15.15hrs I saw this big black cat that was significantly bigger than a Labrador. I saw the side of the animal and it's long u-shaped tail. Even though I was three floors up in my house I got a clear view of the beast and initially felt scared, this eventually turned into excitement. There have been 4 separate sightings of the animal in the last year. At the rear of our property there is a tunnel about 20 metres long, and we think it may be living there. We have not had the courage to go down and investigate. We used to have lots of wild rabbits, now we have none and it seems rather strange." *(Source: Nigel Spencer)*

16th: Oxfordshire/England. Former sceptic George Gasiorowski claims to have spotted the big black cat that is often seen lurking along the hedgerows in the west Oxfordshire area. He was waling home in Church Hamborough along a path which cuts through farmland, near Pinsley Wood at 07.00hrs. It is a route he knows well having walked it for years on his way to the newsagents in Long

Hanborough. He said, "Across the field, near the opening of the wood, there was this black, beautiful animal, about 250 to 300 yards away".

The animal sniffed around before it saw him, then ran away. He added, "I've been very sceptical about this kind of thing, but there it was. It was too big for a domestic cat - about two or three times bigger - and had a long tail, unlike anything I've ever seen on a normal cat. There were very light indentations, and things that were quite obviously deer tracks, but I could definitely see something." *(Source: This is Oxfordshire)*

17th: Cumbria/England. Burton in Kendal resident Alison Flanders spotted a big black cat foraging in a hedgerow while they were driving along an unclassified road from Burton-in-Kendal to Devil's Bridge at Kirkby Lonsdale.

"I know it definitely was not a small cat or a dog," she said, "because it had a tail about three feet long or maybe even longer. It was very dark, it looked like black velvet. It was very lithe and I could imagine it moving very gracefully and slinky". *(Source: Westmorland Gazette)*

circa 18th: County Monaghan/Irish Republic. A local barrister out for a walk came off the beaten track, heard rustling in the bushes and became a little frightened, as whatever it was seemed to be following him, reamining out of sight. He turned, headed back and then heard what he describes as an almighty cat's roar. *(Source: Charlie McGuinness)*

19th : Dorset/England. "I was driving home (to Monkton Wyld) from working at Tescos in Axminster about 5.15 this evening - there were road works in Axminster so I couldn't take my usual route. I took another route which I don't know very well towards the A35, aiming for the turnoff to the west of the one I usually take. I had never actually driven this way before, and I missed the turning. I carried on until I found a small road where I could turn the car round. As I turned into it, I saw a man and an animal further up the road. At first glance it looked like a man taking a dog for a walk. Then I saw that it wasn't a dog. It was difficult to see exactly what colour it was, because the light was behind it, but I think it had some kind of pattern in its coat, maybe stripes, and it seemed to be a dark greyish or brownish colour. I could see its shape quite clearly, and there is no other way to describe it except a very large cat. It was about the size of a small to medium size dog. Then it turned and walked into the hedge. I ran through the possibilities in my mind...dog...fox...deer...but it was the wrong shape for any of them...it wasn't a badger, either......it was definitely cat-shaped. I turned to the friend I was with, and said 'What was that? It looked like a very big cat.' He said ' Maybe he's got the kind of cat you take for walks.' But then we decided that the man probably wasn't taking it for a walk, because of the way it disappeared into the hedge. He seemed to be just looking at it. When I got back home (I live in Monkton Wyld community) I mentioned over dinner that I had seen an exceptionally large cat, and immediately people started talking about urban legends, myths, ghosts and so forth. Until then I had not connected what I had seen with reports of Big Cats in the media.

I'm rather reluctant to report it to the police, as suggested on the *BBC News* website (Warning after 'Big Cat' sighting, 24 Aug 2005) because it didn't seem to be doing any harm, and wasn't at all frightening - it was just walking along quite slowly, first along the road and then into the hedge in the way that animals do around here...It seems a bit unnecessary to hunt it down. However, I did think that it was worth informing you about it. *(Source: sent to Merrily Harpur & Big Cats in Dorset website)*

19th: Sussex/England. Miss D reports: "We were driving along the A2300 by-pass from the A23 towards Burgess Hill (West Sussex). Just before we approached the roundabout (approx 500 yards away) on which the Triangle Leisure Centre is situated, we saw a large dark animal crossing the bridge we were approaching (from left to right) and it was heading towards the farm (locally known as West End Farm). It's shoulders moved like a lions and it didn't look like a cow, horse, dog or cat etc. After going under the bridge we look up again behind us but it appeared to have gone."

The time was 18.00hrs and she further describes the animal as being dark and black/grey coloured. The shape of the ears were not seen. She continued, "as it was crossing a bridge above the road we were driving along and our sighting was obscured by bushes. Definitely saw a large black animal, too big to be a cat from where we were. It would be impossible to see a small animal such as a cat or dog from the road below and there were no people on the bridge to suggest it was a domestic animal."

About 3.5ft in height and 5ft in length. *(Source: BCIB report form)*

20th September: Yorkshire/England. Motorist Jeanette Fill spotted what she thought was possibly a panther during the early hours of the morning. She had her encounter while driving along Deep Lane. She reported: "I was driving from Milnsbridge to Crosland Moor shortly after midnight when I saw this animal. I had my headlights on full beam because it was very dark and I saw it for several seconds. It was standing in the road, clearly profiled, and it was certainly not a large dog. It looked like a very large cat, possibly a black panther, and it didn't move until I pulled alongside. It vanished into the woodland at the side of the road. It certainly scared me."

Jeanette contacted the local police but a quick search of the scene found nothing so the officers left. Later in the day she returned to the spot and found large paw prints in the soft mud leading into woodland. She said, "They were very big and seemed too big for a dog or cat". *(source: Huddersfield Daily Examiner)*

20th: Devon/England. This is the picture of a 'den' that I took last week at

Blackstone rings in South Devon. It was in the ditch of an old iron age fort. Unfortunately, I found it extremely difficult to photograph because of how well hidden it was. There was basically a 30" or so wide circle of flattened sedge that appeared to have been flattened by an animal circling. The field contained sheep, and is regularly visited by the public so I do not think the animal would have used it more than once or twice. This is 1km from a recent sighting and 1km from the sheep kill that I investigated in August. *(Source: Chris Moiser)*

Several dates: Derbyshire/England. At the beginning of the month several lambs were attacked and killed by what locals believed to be the mystery feline predator that frequents the area. Only the skull and spine were left of the lambs. The 'beast' has apparently struck three more times since then, this time on fully grown ewes, and according to the Ripley & Heanor News, "ripping them to pieces." The attacks have taken place on a ten acre stretch of land between Derby Road and Station Road in Denby owned by Matthew Waterfall and John Grace. The fear of further attacks made them sell their remaining stock.

Matthew Waterfall said, "I was brought up in farming and I have never seen anything like this before. I have seen the damage foxes and wild dogs can do to carcasses, but this is nothing like that. These animals have been totally ripped apart by something that is very hungry. I have an open mind as to what could be doing this."

John Grace added, "It's horrific. The beast is getting very brave as it has taken three ewes in a week. These are serious attacks and I am willing to work with anybody that may be able to help resolve these mystery attacks."

Local police constable PC Mick Shaw said, "I am convinced that this has been done by a big cat."

A forensics team were called in to see what they could discover but no results have been published to date. PC Shaw later found a large footprint at the scene which he thought may belong to a large cat. On the 20th of September the Ripley News reported that they may have helped solve the mystery. Over the past week Waingrove residents have spotted two stray Alsatian dogs "racing around nearby fields." They believe these may have been responsible for the attacks. (source: Stephen Sinfield of the Ripley & Heanor News)

23rd: County Monaghan/Irish Republic. (Somewhere on the outskirts of Monaghan Town, County Monaghan, Irish Republic).

20.10hrs

Charlie, McGuinness, John Nutler, Sandy Smith and myself had decided to check out an area where Charlie had informed us there had previous sightings.

It was getting dark, so after parking up on the roadside we each got a torch. Being the last night, they were nearly all out of charge. We never took any other equipment with us (i.e. night vision) as we thought we were just going to have a bit of a recce.

Halfway through the forest we heard horses running and birds taking flight ahead of us.

After successfully negotiating several electric and barbed wire fences, a steep hillock and a boggy forest we emerged at a clearing below us.

We entered the field below whereupon Charlie began to tell us of a sighting which occurred in the exact spot we were stood. Basically a farmer out in his tractor was startled by a large black cat running out of the field on his right, running across his path disappearing into the forest in more or less the same spot that we emerged from it. This occurred in July 2004. Also a dead, partially eaten rabbit was found which may have been eaten by the cat.

At that we heard a rumbling, a pounding, I thought a train, but when my torch lit up about 20 pairs of eyes racing towards us, it took me a little time to realise that the noise was horse's hooves, and the eyes belonged to a herd that was coming our way at a very great speed. Some one shouted "lets get out of here" and we all turned to run. But then Charlie said stop, and when the horses arrived they stopped with inches to spare and he calmed them. Phew, the rest of our hearts were pounding louder then the horse's hooves, as we genuinely thought we were going to be trampled.

We carried on walking along the edge of the field, with the forest to our left, across the field was another row of trees about 200 - 300 yards away.

When we first came into the forest Charlie was a little ahead of us, and he now told us that in front of him he could keep hearing twigs snapping on the forest floor, he could not see what was doing it, only that they seemed to be the same distance away, moving ahead of him, and us in the rear. Before we emerged into the clearing the horses did stampede, I am wondering now what made them stampede and what was breaking the twigs, as whatever it was would have got into the clearing before us.

We reached the far corner of the field and Charlie said "whats that" we looked and all saw greeny/yellow eyes that lit up in our torch beam, as our eyes adjusted we saw that these eyes belonged to a sleek jet-black body that was at least three feet long. It slowly dawned on us we were looking at the Monaghan mystery cat (or one of them), and not only that, it was watching us just as intently. With the light we could only just make it out, but we were certain about what we were seeing. It moved another two or three times but only a few feet.

It then moved slowly to the left and stood with its side to us, with its head turned towards us.

We stood there for about four - five minutes and I suggested that we walk slowly across the field, as our torch-lights were fast fading and we would be seeing nothing, and the stand off was getting us nowhere. As we took about ten steps the cat turned and swiftly shot into the undergrowth behind it.

When we reached the spot we saw that where the cat was stood was a small stream behind it and behind that a barbed wire fence and trees. I looked, I never saw it but John and Sandy did, the cat had not moved far away at all but was stood about 50 feet away. Then it ran off again.

At that point a motorbike roared in the distance, we all momentarily thought it was a roar of a cat, then chuckled. It was at that point I noticed the horses had stopped following us and stood in the middle of the field, it was when we reached them, that they resumed walking behind us all the way to the gate, which again had an electric wire running along it which we only just noticed in time.

It was decided to come back the next day in the light to check for tracks and any signs that the cat may have left. Unfortunately Sandy and I were due to catch the ferry back early the next morning, so the job was left to Charlie and John (we shall update you if there is any more news).

I never saw the cat when I was crouched on the ground, so close yet so far away! But John and Sandy who did describe it as having a big blunt head and its eyes were set about 6-8 inches apart; it turned and ran. I honestly thought it would have left the area by the time we got over there, I should have remembered Lincolnshire.

We headed back to the cars, across the fields, even more electric fences, barbed wire and even more unspeakable things you stand in when its dark. One or two members of the party were still a little apprehensive not wanting to spend any more time in the dark.

What we did see was a cat, I am sure. But I wonder, did it actually walk ahead of us in the forest, making the horses stampede when it reached the clearing ahead of us, crossing the field before us. It was just as interested in us as we were in it, but knew of our presence long before we were aware of it. It obviously showed no aggression, and while not rushing to leave the area, it always kept its distance from us?

Shortly before we went to this area we had checked out woods not far from Charlie's house. We found, at about 7ft up, a set of curious scratches on a beech tree. These were not natural and we could not think of anything that could have made them. They started off with a deep hole, a little wider then the scratch, as if a claw had been dug in, then the scratch marks downwards. Several crossed. *(Mark Fraser personal account)*

25th September: Devon/England. Via Alan White. We got a phonecall yesterday from someone who lives close to Paignton Zoo. He told us that he has heard and also seen what he thinks is a large animal in Clennon Woods. This area runs from the Zoo right down to the ponds and playing areas. This is an extremely large and diverse area both for wildlife and has plenty of cover and hidey holes.

There have been reports of noises from this area before, a keeper said he was sure it was a leopard calling. We, as in Kev and the team, are taking it in shifts and are also putting up a permanent hide which will be accessible from the southern end of the valley. After the weather we have had over the last few days, the area should hopefully be good for prints. *(Source: Alan White)*

26th: Dundee/ Scotland. Coleen McLaren, while driving near the Riverside Recycling Centre at 02.30hrs, was shocked to see a huge cat running across the road in front of her car and away towards nearby houses. She said, "It was probably larger than a dog, it all happened so fast. It went across from one side of the road to another so quickly. It definitely wasn't a normal cat and it didn't move like a dog - it was very lithe in the way it ran across the road." *(Source: Evening Telegraph & Post)*

29th September: Staffordshire/England. An unnamed motorist told the Cheadle Times that, whilst driving along the High Shutt area of Cheadle, he spotted a large black cat at around 18.30hrs. When he saw the cat, which was about the size of a collie dog, he pulled up on the side of the road just in time to see the animal "slink across a field and then disappear into a hedgerow."

The witness continued: "I would say I watched it for about a minute or so, it was slinky like a cat, it had a long tail. It was feline all right and it didn't seem to be in any hurry, but then it went into a hedgerow and disappeared."

Local police stressed that it is illegal to try and shoot a wildcat. Last month a number of shooters apparently were conducting night time hunts in search for the big cat on the moorlands. *(source: Cheadle Times)*

September 2005: Northamptonshire/England. Email via Matt Dumont of Northamptonshire Big Cats.

Mat reports via the UK Big Cat Mailing list: "We have very recently had a report on www.big-cats.co.uk regards warning notices in a Northamptonshire village, Church Brampton. This follows a report of a convincing sighting last month: 'Hi, There are numerous warning notices around my area (church Brampton - Northants). I am concerned about my family while we are horse riding/cycling are we in any danger? If you ignore these cats will they ignore you? please advise. Thanks'"

As I have not visited the area for a while, I'm not certain of the validity of the report. I have followed it up by asking if they were official warnings (ie: police), but will investigate further this week.

For the record, Church Brampton is surrounded by two golf clubs and a local wood (Harlestone Firs - a number of sightings have been reported here since 1999). A working quarry is also only 2 miles away.

Mat further reports: "I have now been up to the area and can confirm that the notices have been put up (not officially but by a big cat investigator). It seems someone has spotted two pumas walking across the golf course in the village. This follows on from a report I have received from a resident who spotted a 'panther' in the lane leading to the same golf course.

I did a brief investigation of the local area, I know it myself very well and will continue to monitor it closely." *(source: Matt Dumont of Northamptonshire Big Cats)*

OCTOBER

3rd: Dorset/England. At approx 9.30 am on Monday 3/10/05 I was driving down Giddy Lake in Wimborne. I was looking from my right to my left admiring the properties when I spotted what I shortly afterwards described as a Labrador sized black cat in an overgrown area of woodland. It had an angular shaped head and was sitting on its haunches. I stopped the car and backed up to see the creature for a few seconds, before it seemed to lift into the air in a pounce like movement and disappeared into the brambles and bushes. My brother, who was with me in the car, is not as convinced as I am as to what I saw, but he did not have as clear a view as me. I am not from this area and knew nothing of the so called Dorset Cat. It was the description of another sighting as a Labrador sized cat that made me write this, as that was exactly as I described it. *(Source: Merrily Harpur)*.

circa 4th: Renfrewshire/Scotland. Two workmen spotted what they claimed to be a black leopard in Auchenbothie, Port Glasgow Road, Kilmacolm. The 'leopard' approached the work van quite close, while they were sat in it, affording them a very good look at the animal. *(Source: The Greenock Telegraph)*

4th: Fife/Scotland. I received several telephone calls from various members of the press regarding the finding of a large print by police officers in Balbirnie Woods, Markinch. Unfortunately I was having problems receiving the copies via email, and could not open them. After the initial excitement the pictures, when they finally came through, were a bit of a let down, as they looked to me like dog. Anyway the story is as follows.

Fife police officers and SSPCA officials conducted a search of the woods, up to ten in total. They found a print measuring 10cm by 9cm which they confirmed (via their expert, although no name was given) that it was believed to have been left behind by a "large cat-like creature." Mark Maylin, wildlife officer for Fife police, reported: "We have a duty to protect the public from what could be a dangerous animal. We searched woodland adjacent to Balbirnie park and found a number of paw prints, which do appear to be from a big cat. The next step is to try to find and capture the animal and have it re-located in an environment that is safer, both for it and the public. Based on the number of reports over recent years there could be as many as half a dozen in Fife alone. The lynx was originally native to Scotland and would have no trouble surviving in the wild."

I need to see the original casts before I can reach a firm conclusion, but my feeling at the moment is that they belong to a biggish dog. *(Source: Fife Fee Press: Fife Police)*

4th: Dundee/Scotland. Russell Girling from Dundee fears that the mystery cat often seen in the area is responsible for the disappearance of his pet cat. The cat went missing over a week ago, shortly after two sightings of the big cat in the area. Mr Girling was disturbed in his sleep when his cat Oscar went beserk in the kitchen. He went downstairs and opened his back door, and saw in the garden an unusual beast. He said, "I've never seen anything that big. It was very quick, it just leapt away over the back wall of the garden—I'd say it was at least the size of a Labrador." *(Source: The Dundee Courier)*

5th: Dorset/England. (sighting by big cat investigator Merrily Harpur). Ahem - I saw a big cat on Sunday night! It was just as bad as my first sighting about 10 years ago - very fleeting. Worse, because this cat was very small for a big cat, about the size of my neighbours' Springer spaniel bitch. Worse still, it did not cross in front of me but in front of someone else, so I don't really count it as a sighting - not compared to everyone else's long leisurely looks at huge felines. But anyway; I had stopped at the Blandford roundabout and was looking at a car about to enter the roundabout from the next road right when I saw a cat on the verge next to it recoil and then run across the road in front of it. My first assumption was of a 'normal' cat of course, but as it ran across the road I saw its whole body in silhouette, back-lit by the other car's headlights, and I realised this was no moggy. It was spaniel-sized, but longer, and it had the shape and musculature of a big cat. Don't ask me what it was! Just like the last sighting, this one took place when I was nearing home after driving all day, and was tired.

So they could both say something about me rather than ABCs! This was about 9pm and no, I didn't get out - I was in a stream of traffic going round a large roundabout. It would have meant driving about half a mile before I could stop, parking the van and then walking back. Something told me there would be no point in this! Also, as I say, I was tired and dying to get home, and couldn't be bothered.

When I spotted it, it was on the flat, mown grass verge right by the kerb. The roundabout was at the edge of town, with woods and fields on one side of it and the town on the other - it was crossing towards the town. As I said, it was looking away from me and towards the car approaching it, and drawing back as if wondering whether to cross or not. *(Source: Merrily Harpur)*

6th: Leicestershire/England. I have spoken to a lady from the Oakham area at length, and her sighting seems not to be one of the usual suspects (i.e dog/ fox/ badger or domestic).

She was driving at 06:50 on the narrow Burley water tower to Exton road (NE of Oakham) near the Rutland Falconry centre when she suddenly saw this massive cat on the side of the road. It was crouching, and leapt up vertically ("like it was on springs"[1]), clearing the 6 foot hedge into the adjacent field bordering the massive, ancient Burley woods.

The thing she noticed most was its very long, thick tail. The animal appeared black in colour.

The area has many woods, and Burley woods are massive, full of herds of deer as well as smaller muntjac etc. There have been scores of sightings within ½ mile of this one, although none this year to my knowledge.

A spectacular sighting on nearby Barnsdale Avenue, Exton occured about 5 years ago, when a party of teenagers and teachers on a school field trip saw a panther-like cat chase and kill a full grown deer buck which, understandably, left them all very distressed. *(Source: Nigel Spencer)*

6th: Rutland/England. Last night at 10.15 I saw a black panther walking close to the hedgerow in South Luffenham in Rutland. I am in no doubt about what I saw, I am still so excited nearly 24 hours later. *(Source: Unnamed witness via Nigel Spencer)*

7th: Gloucestershire. England. 17.45 hours. I was a passenger in a car travelling on the M25 from Gatwick to Leicestershire approx 5 minutess from Chel-

---

[1] Many people in the UK have described this "coiled spring "action in the past, and it is typical behaviour. Both Pumas and Panthers have enormous power in their legs allowing them to jump considerable heights form a standing start; security fences etc. are cleared with ease.

tenham turn off in a traffic queue. The cat was standing still, tail carried in curve with right foot raised looking straight ahead cat was in front of a woodland at back of field sighting very clear it was not a large domestic cat it was not a dog it was a black leopard/panther type animal clearly visible daylight only just beginning to get dusk. *(Source: BCIB report form)*

7th: Buckinghamshire/England. A black panther-like animal was seen at Ashley Green, Chesham, Bucks, crossing the road towards the village hall at 7.20 a. m. *(Source: Nigel Spencer)*

7th: Cambridgeshire/England. The witness reports: "It looked like a black puma - side view for a few seconds as it walked out of the darkness across a well lit path into long grass - size: height about the same as a medium size dog, but longer - methodical walking." The cat was spotted at St Botolph Green, Orton Longueville at a distance of about 70 metres away. *(Source: Matt Dumont)*

7th: Lothians/Scotland. Around 18.00hrs a Border Collie, Jude, belonging to Richard Brown scented an animal and gave chase towards Henderson's Agricultural Centre in Haddington. The animal it was chasing was described as a big cat, and cleared a 10ft chain link fence "with apparent ease." It headed off towards the old A1 road and the Garleton Hills.

Mr Brown said, "I'm glad my dog didn't tangle with the animal as I fear it could it would have come off worse. I had gone out of the house about 5.45am to put the bin out for the refuse men when I noticed what appeared to be a large black dog crossing the road.

The dog obviously caught its scent and went after it at great speed as though she knew she was chasing a big cat. There was no sound and the animal took off. It leapt the fence and I saw its black shape and a long black tail. I don't believe it was a deer and it did not have the bushy tail of a fox. It was definitely a panther-like animal." *(Source: East Lothian Courier)*

9th: Renfrewshire/Scotland. As I was making my way home I was driving on the Quarry Road making for the Kilmacolm Bridge of Weir Road. As I approached this road I noticed a big cat in the field. I stooped the car and I could not believe what I was looking at but it defiantly was a leopard it just walked by as if I was not there and disappeared onto the cycle track. The witness describes the cat as "half as big as a dog" although what species of dog is not mentioned, black, 3ft in length. It was around 20ft away and the witness observed it for about 15-20 seconds. *(Source: BCIB report form)*

15th: Lancashire/England. A large black cat was spotted by a female witness in the Huyton area. She described it as having a very long tail and eyes that "stood out." *(Source: Christopher Johnston)*

10th: Anglesey/Wales. 21.30hrs. Llanddona, Beaumaris, Anglesey. Labrador-sized black cat. I was walking down my garden path with a small torch which gave just enough light to see where I was placing my feet. Suddenly and without any warning and in complete silence, the cat leaped through the beam of my torch and vanished. As I have stated, the cat was labrador sized. It went passed me at about chest height in a single bound. I got no details other than a clear impression of size. I am positive of what it was because I have had a number of previous sightings in the immediate vicinity of my house and land in good light conditions.

This witness has had four sightings over the years. *(Source: BCIB report form)*

10th: Cheshire/England. Approximately 12:30 pm. Runcorn. Whilst walking my dog past Runcorn town hall, I looked towards the town hall car park. I think I spotted a large, black jaguar-like (!!!!)) animal walking behind the bushes. It was walking fairly slowly but I only looked at it in time to see the back half of the animal. I would estimate it to be about the size of a labrador (maybe slightly larger) and had powerful looking hindquarters. I own a large black Great Dane and its tail was longer and much thicker than my dog's. It did not walk like a dog. Its legs were very muscular and (although I only saw the rear of it) it appeared to be very chunky/stocky. I think my dog may have spotted it earlier than I did as he was looking in that direction for a while. I was going to walk up into the car park to investigate my sighting further but to be perfectly honest, I was too scared!

I don't mind you contacting me about this but I would rather you did not release any of my details - I don't want people to think I am some kind of crank!!

The witness further describes the tail as: "Long, thick (different to a dog's), hanging down but curled slightly at the end so the last few inches were nearly parallel to the ground. *(Source: BCIB report form)*

circa 13th: Hertfordshire/England. Sarah Adams and her daughter were walking her Jack Russell terriers in a field off Bowers Heath Lane, Harpenden. They saw a big black cat crouched on a hill ahead of them. Sarah's daughter Ellie got close enough to see that the cat had yellow eyes, before they scooped up their dogs and ran home. Sarah said, "We always take our dogs up the fields and have been doing it for the past 20 years but I have never seen anything like that before."

When they first saw the animal 50 yards away they thought it was a dog, as they got closer they stared in amazement. She added, "It was watching us as we came up the hill but we carried on because I was thinking I hope it isn't a dog injured." When her daughter suggested it might be a wolf, they picked up the dogs and turned to run back. Sarah continued, "I find it difficult to run very far and as I was looking around, it was still crouched down and moving as though it was prowling. It had pointed ears and a very round face and it was much bigger than a large Rottweiler. I didn't see if it had a tail but it was black with a very long body and was crawling along the ground." *(Source: Herts Advertiser)*

14th: Stirlingshire/Scotland. 4.45pm. Stenhousemuir. I was walking along the road, adjacent to the field when I saw what I thought at first was a dog. I stood and watched for a while and as I stood, I noticed this was not a dog. Its tail was far too long and it moved in a very cat-like way, although too big to be a domestic cat. I ran home to get my camera but when I got back I couldn't find it and did not want to chance entering the field in case what I had saw was a big cat of some sort. It was bouncing around like it was on the hunt, and would lay low in the grass and then pounce, perhaps for rabbits. The witness further describes the animal as being black, with a tail much longer than that of a dog, and longer then the rest of its body. A meter in length not including the tail. *(Source: BCIB report form)*

15th: Darlington/England. A large black cat was spotted in a local farmer's headlights on the outskirts of Hartlepool. Location: between the A1 and A19 east to west, and Trimdon and Stockton north to south, is the third main area where big cats are reported in the north east. *(Source: Ian Bond)*.

16th: Highland/Scotland. While walking back to the Durnoch Caravan Park Alan Herbert spotted what he said looked "something like a panther" on the Struie golf course at around midnight. The animal was 100 yards away, and Mr Herbert was a little unnerved when he saw it. He said it was bigger than an Alsatian, and it just stared at him. He made a noise to frighten the animal off but it never moved and continued to stare. When Mr Herbert began walking again the animal then ran off. *(Source: The Northern Times)*

16th: Lancashire/England. A man was driving along a narrow road with fields either side. The road is on moss land, so it is very uneven and you have to drive slowly. While driving down the road a big black cat actually jumped over his bonnet.

The farm where he saw the cat has had droppings left near to the farm house and they have been left there on three occasions, all left uncovered. I have attached two pictures of some the farmer collected for me to look at. They look brown in the picture but they were black. I had nothing on me to measure them but they were quite big and were segmented. You can see small fragments of bone in them, but when I broke them open there was no hair inside. One interesting thing was that as I was walking to the car with them in a plastic bag a dog had run off from its owner. He was trying to call it back. As it came onto the road it ran to me and was going crazy to get the bag off me, he kept sniffing the contents. I am not sure about these with there being no hair, but thought you all would like to have look. *(Source: Christopher Johnston)*

16th: Aberdeenshire/Scotland. Mark and Diane Allan were heading for Burn-

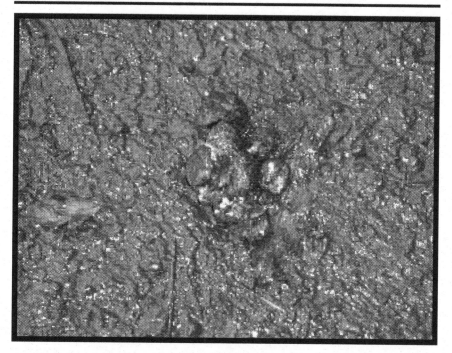

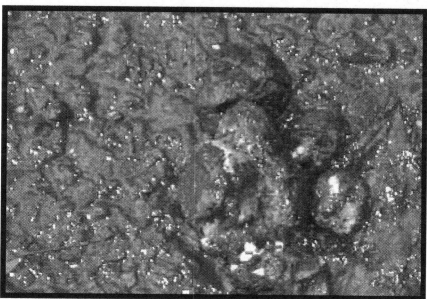

Big cat droppings? left near to the farm house, Lancashire.

hervie, Inverurie, when a big cat wandered into the middle of the road. Mr Allan first thought the animal was a cat or a dog as it walked towards them, when it changed direction and bounded over a ditch they realised that the animal was definitely feline, beige in colour with pointed ears. The sighting took place on the road from the Miller's at Midmar to Sauchen, and has now convinced the couple of the existence of big cats in the area. Mr Allan said, "We've seen big cats in the flesh in Africa, and this was like something you would meet over there. It was good to see one like that because you hear so many stories about sightings around Bennachie and not that far from where we saw it."

He added, "We've got three Labradors and when I first saw the thing walking along the road I thought it was about the same size. But when it turned side-on, it was obviously a cat and had a bit of a fluffy tail, like a cross between a big mountain cat and a puma. There were no leopard spots or tiger markings, but the tail was curled at the tip and it had large paws. Beige and with pointed ears, the animal took the roadside ditch in one leap and easily cleared a stone dyke as well.

The way it jumped was just like a cat, and I thought I saw a twinkle in its eye as it looked at us. That could have been markings around its eyes like you might find on a cat".

On the same night Beth Duff from Midmar reported that her horses were very "spooked" at around the same time as the couple's sighting. She said, "Their behaviour struck me as unusual - and I believe it could have been caused by the presence of a predator. *(Source: Aberdeen Press & Journal)*

circa 17th: Aberdeenshire/Scotland: Police launched a search for a mystery predator that slaughtered 15 sheep in the Drumdale area near Huntly. Police said that there is no evidence as yet to suggest a big cat was involved. This area saw similar kills in 2001, which were was put down to the cat often seen in the area which is known as the 'Beast of Bin'. *(Source: Aberdeen Press & Journal).*

17th: Worcestershire/England. 06.00 - 06.30hrs. Culverness Farm Clows Top nr Kidderminster. Two large black cats the size of a springer spaniel, 2 half feet long to 3 feet long, 18 inches to 2 feet high. "My dogs acted strange and were sniffing round the farm yard, and went off down the field towards a dingle then came running back towards me.

I walked down the field and the dogs followed very sheepishly. As I came to a new clearing that I had recently made down by the brook, the two black cats where mee-awing at each other about 6ft apart. They saw me and the dogs and then ran off hunched low back in to the wood.
A farmer about half a mile from me has found lamb carcases up a tree not long ago." *(Source: BCIB report form).*
18th: Dorset/England. 10-year old Nicholas Rogers from Poole got the shock

of his life when returning home for his tea. As he ran from the recreation ground to Silverdale Close he saw a large black animal crossing the road towards him. He slowed to a walk and crossed over the road coming to within 8ft of the animal, which stopped in the road and turned to look at Nicholas. He described the animal as a cat the size of a Labrador "with a large strange shaped head and yellow eyes." It then turned and ran into bushes; Nicholas did the same and ran home.

His mother said, "He's a sensible boy and not given to flights of fancy. I think he was a little scared when he got home. We have a cat at home, but he said the creature he saw was at least twice as big with a very smooth black coat." *(Source: Daily Echo)*

18th: Cheshire/England. This paw print was photographed in Bollington Cheshire on 18th October 2005. This date coincided with the vicious slaughter of a fully grown sheep in the field next to our house on the same day. *(Source: Brian Peacock)*

18th: Bedfordshire/England. A lynx-like cat spotted off Windermere Drive in Biggleswade. *(source: Luton Today)*

20th: Bedfordshire /England. Terence Gilliland believes he spotted a lynx prowling in his garden late at night in Lime Tree Walk, Biggleswade. He said, "I saw a movement and thought it was an ordinary cat at first but it jumped on the shed roof and stood facing the light. It's eyes were lit up like headlights and I was amazed because it had got a very small face and two big ears that stood vertically upright and were pointed at the top." *(Source: Luton Today)*

20th: Leicestershire/England. "Just a tentative enquiry, have you received any reports of big cats in the last couple of weeks in the Cropston/Woodhouse area of Leicestershire? I believe I had a sighting at about 05.30, on the road-side just above the junction of the road to Woodhouse Eaves and the road from Cropston. A large black cat was sat on the verge, as I approached it looked towards the car and got up. Then I saw that it had large tail, curved almost to the floor. It effortlessly jumped approx a 4ft wall into small wooded area. *(Source: Nigel Spencer)*

20th: Devon/England. Following up on the cat sighting last week (Wednesday morning) between Sharkham Point and Berry Head. The lady was out walking her dog when she spotted a large black cat in the field adjacent to where they where they were. She described the cat as being long and sleek, with a long sweeping tail. When members of our team talked to her they showed her some photos and mock ups and she picked out a black leopard. She told them both that the cat seemed to be searching the base of the hedges as if looking for something. It went through the hedge and disappeared. She said, "Kevin checked the other side to where the cat was and he told me that there is a path on and across the other side of the road leading to Sharkham Point and he believes that the cat may have taken this route. This sighting is only about 5 minutes walk from the sighting I had the January before last, of where I described the cat as being in transition between cub and adult." *(Source: Alan White)*

21st: Aberdeenshire/Scotland. Motorists travelling on the Crossroads to Craigievar road stopped in their tracks when a large black cat ran across the road. Tarland resident Aileen Longino was on her way to Alford, followed by her sister in another car, when a driver hailed them to stop. Mrs Longino thought they had stopped because of an accident, but looked towards the field where the man was pointing and was shocked to see a leopard! She said, "The man was very shaken and when I looked across to the field, I could see why. There was a large black cat walking across it. It looked around a metre tall and was very powerful-looking. It had a long tail which was curled at the tip and had a few kinks in it. The field had been cut, the hay was in bales, so the cat stood out very vividly against the yellow colour of the ground. My sister had a camera in the boot of her car but there was no chance for us to take pictures. The cat began walking towards us at one point and it was safest for us to stay in our cars because we had four children between us, two in each car .We were stopped on a piece of road where it could have been unsafe for us all to stay there, so we had to drive off.

I didn't ask his name and, when we came back a while later, there was no sign of the cat or anyone else. He had spoken about reporting it to the police, and I wondered if anybody else witnessed it. There had just been our three cars and a post van which also arrived, but we didn't all stay around.". *(Source: Aberdeen Press & Journal)*

21st: Wester Ross/Scotland. What is believed to be a large black cat was caught on CCTV outside of DMK motors on the outskirts of Lochcarron. Garage owner Donnie McKenzie was surprised to see the animal on the tape the next morning. Mr McKenzie reported to the West Highland Free Press that he was "not sure what it was", but showed the footage to TV presenter Terry Nutkins when he came in to have his car serviced. Mr Nutkins said, "he was excited by the prospect of the mystery creature - which resembles either a panther or a puma - roaming the Wester Ross Hills. It's very interesting to say the least, what I could make out certainly looked bigger than a domestic cat. It was covering a large manhole and I'd say it was at least three feet long. It looked very low, very heavy and very black. I'm always rather sceptical and don't like to get too romantic about these kind of things but this has definitely sparked my interest. There was something different about this cat.

I'd really like to see if it would make another appearance. I've been living in the Highlands for many years and never heard of anything like it."

The footage apparently shows the animal walking past a three-and-a-half foot long manhole cover. It is described as being black and having a lengthier head and neck than most domestics.

Mr McKenzie believes that they may have caught the animal on CCTV last year, but it was too indistinct to make out. *(Source: West Highland Free Press)*

22nd: Worcestershire/England. Thursday 22nd Oct 2005. At 15.45 in good daylight. Landranger No. 150 cat at ref 853428. Seen from 852428 (approx).

Party of 4 adults and children in pushchairs (no alcohol had been taken). None of us given to flights of fancy. We were downwind and closer to the river, where two paths meet. Cat walked towards us over a slight brow, as if unaware of us at first (briefly). then stopped about 50 yards away, sat back and regarded us for about 1-2 minutes, before calmly standing and walking into the woods beside the path. We had time to watch it through binoculars.

Cat was brown with black face and tail, we thought it more puma-like colouring, until we saw it's face properly. Closer view through the binoculars showed the very black, "pug-featured" face, like a black leopard. Size- We thought it was a very big German shepherd dog at first, but it's walk was too cat-like. As it finally left, it's tail was like a leopard's in shape.

We had earlier found bones of a sheep's leg on the bridle path we walked (still with feet attached), and a lot of wool in a copse nearby. Local farmer told us he had lost "the odd lamb". *(Source: Witness report via Nigel Spencer)*

23rd: Dundee/Scotland. Monifieth Town Council. Ian Mortimer was walking his dog along Monifieth Beach at around 20.00hrs. He was beside the football pitches next to the caravan park when he spotted a strange animal "struggling to get through a fence". He said, "It was definitely not a normal cat. It was about three times the size of a household cat and it certainly wasn't a dog. It was about the size of a collie dog but moved like a cat.

I was about 20 to 30 yards away from it when I saw it struggle to get through the wooden slats of the fence by the path. Eventually it jumped over the fence and slumped on to the ground and disappeared in to the long grass. There are lots of deer and rabbits in the area and it did seem to be a well-fed animal." *(Source: Dundee Courier)*

circa 24th: Lancashire/England. A large black cat has been spotted round a garden pond several times. The owner has installed cameras in the hope of catching the animal on film. The cat is described as being jet-black, 2ft high, 6ft long with a long tail and a white chest. *(Source: Christopher Johnston)*

27th: Staffordshire/England. A large cat said to be a black panther was spotted in the High Shutt area of Cheadle. A motorist driving towards Cheadle at around 18.00hrs spotted the cat which he estimated to be about the size of a collie dog.

He pulled up by the side of the road and watched the animal "slink across a field then disappear into a hedgerow".

The motorist told the Cheadle Times: "I would say I watched it for about a minute or so, it was slinky like a cat, it had a long tail. It was feline all right and it didn't seem to be in any hurry, but then it went into a hedgerow and disappeared." *(Source: Cheadle Times)*

27th: Hampshire/England. 19.00hrs. We live in very rural Hampshire. I had arrived home and was walking towards house & heard cats screaming very loud. I ran towards the front of the house. My children said our cat ran thru the cat flap to inside the house. Outside the cat flap I saw this large brown cat, I screamed, it looked at me and ran into our field. Our other pet cat disappeared. Further described as big as a small Labrador but shaped like a tabby domestic although with a much bigger and fatter body with a smallish head. *(Source: BCIB report form)*

28th: Aberdeenshire/Scotland "We recently saw what we are sure were kittens of the Kellas cats, in the woods above Glenlivet school. We had never heard of this species but when we saw them my daughter commented how their heads looked like rabbit heads. Our dog chased them and they shot up to the top of a large fir tree. *(Source: BCIB report form)*

circa31st: Dorset/England. I have been told of a couple of sightings of big cats in the Blandford area. One of my colleagues was out with his wife on the disused railway line at the rear of Hopegood Close in Charlton Marshall near Blandford, when they spotted a big black cat. He says it was too big to be a domestic cat and they had a good look for a couple of minutes before it moved off. I understand it was earlier this week. Needless to say, he now takes his digital camera with him in the hope of getting a picture. Unfortunately most of our other work colleagues have been taking the rise out of him, but it did prompt someone else to tell me of a sighting last year. He and his wife were looking out of a kitchen window in a house on Dorchester Hill near Bryanstone, Blandford, when they both saw a large black cat crossing a nearby field. Both areas are fairly close to one another, so it could be the same cat. *(Source: Merrily Harpur)*

circa 31st: Yorkshire/England. Several sightings of a big black cat in the Halifax area around Cunnery Wood at Hipperholme and near Park Road, Elland. Police are taking the sightings seriously and investigating the reports. *(Source: Yorkshire Today)*

NOVEMBER

1st: Angus/Scotland. A Dundee woman saw a large black cat dart out in front of her car on Riverside Drive. *(source: Dundee Courier)*

1st: Yorkshire/England. Healey Green Lane, Huddersfield, a woman who wishes not to be named was driving along at 10.30 pm when she saw what she was convinced was a big cat. It was walking up the side of the road that she was driving down. Its head was at about the same level as the car, and she described the animal as having smooth fur, and moving like "big cats do".

The following day Kieron McElhatton was out walking his dog at Berry Brow at about 1.30pm when he saw "a very large cat". He told the newspaper, "It stopped and looked at me and I got a clear sight. It was something like a puma." Unfortunately no further description of the animal is given. *(source: Huddersfield Daily Examiner)*

circa 3rd Devon/England. Daniel Herbert 12, and Jordan Rowe, 13, were building a tree house in Barnstaple's Rock Park, when they had a terrifying encounter. They found "black fur" and saw what they said were claw marks on the bark of the tree. Jordan said, "We heard a growling noise and we went down to see what it was. We could see it (the big cat) in the grass. It had the head of a panther." The animal was only about 6ft away from them. They described the tail as being about 3ft long. Apparently at that, they ran, dropping the fur as they went. It was unfortunate that BCIB did not hear about the incident until over a month later when the chance of finding any hard evidence was impossible. Members in the area could have gone straight to the scene.

Christopher Johnston subsequently met one of the lads and said, "The boy I talked to was a very level headed young man and described a big cat to me very well. He had had some stick at school because of it, I think his mum just wanted to forget about it and have no more to do with it, but I understand that." *(source: Chris Johnston)*

circa 4th: Angus Scotland. A West End, Dundee man fears that a big cat may have eaten his pet cat. Russell Girling saw a large black cat in his back garden along Newhall Gardens. He was disturbed from his sleep early in the morning after his cat, Oscar, began making a racket in the kitchen. Mr. Girling went outside to investigate and "saw an unusual beast", he said, "I've never seen anything that big. It was very quick, it just leapt away over the back wall of the garden. I'd say it was at least the size of a Labrador." Now his cat has been missing for over two weeks and he believes it may be a victim of the big cat.

5th: Leicestershire/England. The Leicestershire Fire and Rescue CEO spotted what she believes was a large black cat on Humble Lane, Cossington on Charnwood. The cat ran along the side of her car "on the narrow lane by the Sheffield railway". The witness straight away reported the incident to the police.

Nigel Spencer reports: "Interestingly there have been a lot of reports at that location, both on the road and by train drivers on the railway itself (stopped at signals). One sighting the other year involved two ex-police officers on a nighttime farm-watch patrol on two separate nights. They were on VHF to the police and radioed it in as well but as there was no perceived threat the force did not attempt a lock-down, or launch a helicopter, unlike some places!" *(source: Nigel Spencer, Rutland and Leicestershire Panther Watch)*

10th: Devon/England. Delivery driver, Cedric Munslow came face-to-face with a large black cat at around 07.00 hrs as he was driving along the lane at Dunchideock, West of Exeter.

The cat just "suddenly" walked across the road, forcing Mr. Munslow to slam hard on his brakes stopping just five yards from the animal. He said, "It was huge, much bigger than your average pet cat – about five feet long and three feet high. The thing was so big, it managed to cross the road in just three leaps. It went up the bank on the other side of the road, turned round and looked straight at me, and then disappeared into the gorse. I was not scared because I was in my van, but there was no way I was going to get out, not likely. It was no ordinary cat, it was big. I would not want to get a blow-out down there, that would be too scary, now I know that thing is about." *(source: Western Morning News)*

10th: Devon/England. Several hours after Mr. Munslow's sighting another sighting was reported two miles away. The witness rang Gemini radio to report the incident. *(source: Western Morning News)*

circa 10th: County Monaghan/Irish Republic. At the exact spot, or rather field, on the outskirts of Monaghan where we had our last sighting in September, the land owner saw a strange animal. As before, he had just come out of the woods, the horses were spooked by something and he saw a large black "strange looking animal as big as a Labrador" run away into the opposite copse. The farmer is not saying that it was a big cat, but does believe that it wasn't a dog, and that he hasn't seen an animal like it before. He wasn't aware of our previous sighting. *(source: Charlie McGuinness)*

11th: Dorset/England. "I'm writing to report a sighting of what I believe to have been a black panther, just inside Wareham Forest, near Wareham, Dorset, late on night of 11th November 2005.

I was sitting reading at home, when my 6 month old German Shepherd heard a noise at about 11.30pm and then became very on edge. I thought he might have heard people coming back from the pub, or maybe a local fox or stag, but after 10 minutes of unsettled behaviour I decided to let him outside into the back garden, which is enclosed by a 6ft fence all round. He went out, stood there, sniffed a bit and then turned on his tail and came back inside very quickly.

I didn't think any more of this until about midnight when I let him outside before I went to bed. As I always do, I made him sit by the inner porch door and wait while I opened the outer door and checked that it was ok for him to go outside. The moment I opened the front door, I immediately saw this large black shadow on the driveway. It was late and I was tired, so for a split second my rational mind registered this as a large black cat sitting or resting on the driveway with a huge black shadow making it look bigger. But as I opened the door I saw it begin to get up and I realised that there was no shadow and this was no ordinary cat.

Whatever our nationality or culture, we all have an instinctive knowledge of "danger", and at that point all my courage left me. Instinctively, I immediately called my poor young dog, who rushed to the door, took one look at the creature and began to leap towards it. The big cat immediately responded by turning and taking one huge leap into the copse a few feet behind it, on the other side of the driveway. It was then that I saw just how big it was. It was much too big for a cat, the size of a working Labrador, but with the litheness, confidence and thickness of leg of a panther. My dog chased the cat into the copse and I heard him growl a very cautious warning growl (at least I assumed at the time it was him), quite unlike anything I have heard him make before.

At that point my dog came rushing back inside. Tonight, he has been very cautious about going outside again and steers clear of the area where the "panther" was sitting. I have to admit, I've been very cautious before opening the front door!

I checked for footprints in the copse and found only large footprints which I took to be my dog's. The ground there is covered in soft earth and leaves at the moment which makes identification difficult." *(source: unnamed witness, via Merrily Harpur)*

13th: Dumbartonshire/Scotland. A hunter came across prints 3inches across, no claw marks and rounded, rather than "tear-drop" pad. The find was not far from Helensborough, or from where there is thought to be a black dog running wild. It allegedly killed 100 sheep in a night not far from where he was. *(source: Brian Murphy)*

14th: Somerset/England. "We saw on Monday a Panther with a young cub, the cub was the size of a small terrier. I own a farm outside Weston-super-mare, near the A370 Hewish, and a number of people have seen this cat. Would it be hard to set a cage and catch this cat? I believe this cat lives on the Puxton Moor." *(source: Nigel Spencer – Rutland & Leicestershire Panther Watch)*

19th: Northamptonshire/England. At the River Nene hump-back bridge, nr. Wansford, Peterborough, at 12.17pm (Saturday). The colour was dark brown/lighter brown under the body. It had rounded ears and a very long tail which was touching the ground. It appeared to be very muscular and was the height and length of an Alsatian dog. Whilst fishing o the River Nene near Wansford with a friend. I looked into the field opposite where I was fishing and noticed an animal eating something. I never really took much notice as animals are usually grazing when we are fishing. This animal then raised its head and I realised that it was a big cat, a Puma! I shouted to my friend in the next fishing peg to look but as he got up the cat ran off along the hedgerow and jumped a small fence. *(source: Colin Northern via BCIB report form)*

21st: Ceredigion/Wales. Armed police were called to a farm in the Dihewyd area, after a partly-devoured sheep's carcass was discovered and a large black cat was seen on two consecutive nights. Sgt. Phil Edwards said that the police were taking the incidents very seriously and a forensic examination of the carcase would be taking place. "We had a report from a farmer in the Dihewyd area that a sheep had been killed on Thursday night, and that he had seen a very large and fast animal while he was walking his dog". Sgt Edwards said. *(source: Cardigan Today)*

22nd: Carmarthenshire/Wales. An off duty police officer spotted a large cat at around 5.40pm in the Ladies Walk area. He said it is around 2ft tall and 3ft long, with brown fur, an extended neck and a flat squashed face. The daily post reports: "Sergeant Huw Griffiths of Port Talbot police, said: "We went there and managed to get a plaster cast of one of the prints. It is certainly bigger than that of any dog.' Asked if it might prove the big cat's existence, he said: "Absolutely. It is not that we did not believe the reports from the public but we do not know them personally. This time it was one of our own officers. We are bringing in an expert from Aberystwyth University to study the plaster cast. There is also a hair in the cast, which we did not know about at the time, so that will be sent off for examination too.'" *(source: This is South Wales)*

Not long after this the police issued another statement announcing that analysis had revealed the cast and hair "do not belong to a puma but either to a lynx or a mountain lion", and they warned people not to approach the animal under any circumstances. *(source: This is South Wales)*

It is not mentioned in any reports who the experts on Wild Cats were, nor why they could not distinguish between a Mountain Lion and a Lynx, whose DNA apparently cannot be confused. Acting Superintendent Mike Mantripp said, "It has not harmed anyone and it seems to be quite afraid of people". However, he continued that people should be aware that it was a wild animal and should not be approached, and that people should not go out hunting for it as this was only likely to lead to further problems.

After reading these reports Chris Moiser, scientific advisor to the BCIB and the CFZ said, "The DNA result is hard to comprehend, the puma (aka mountain lion) has DNA almost as far apart from the Lynx as it is possible to get in the cat family. Yet it could be one or the other according to this report! The police witness describes an animal about 2 feet high and 30 ins long, and yet describes a footprint bigger than that of any dog – a cat of that size would not produce a footprint that big. I have also personally met a large breed of dog with feet bigger than those of a Puma.

The footprint cast is said to "clearly" show "large claws", much larger than those of any domestic cat. This is very unlike a cat footprint – All cats (except the Cheetahs, and those dying of tetanus) have retractable claws. If there is any doubt as to whether the animal seen was a Lynx or a Mountain Lion perhaps the Mark 1 eyeball test could be employed – if the witness says that it had a long tail it is a Mountain Lion, if it has a very short tail it is a Lynx.! (cheaper than DNA work too!). How convenient that hair was found in the plaster, and that it was fit for DNA testing, I have never heard of this before."

The Welsh Assembly stepped in and sent a member of the Assembly Government Wildlife Management Unit who reported that "there was no hair from the animal available from which to take a DNA sample. The paw print plaster cast is of poor quality and unlikely to prove the existence of a big cat." It ended with the statement that "there has been no confirmation a big cat is at large in the Baglan area."

On the 6th December the police backtracked their claims that the evidence found belonged to a big cat. Divisional Commander Cliff Filer reported in the South Wales Evening Post that the test results were "inconclusive", and that there had been no confirmed sightings.

Comments on the icWales website:

"I saw this animal next to the motorway about a year ago. It was sitting on a ledge and it had tufted ears. I told my husband about it and thought no more about it until I saw this article. I didn't even know there was a mystery about it. I just thought that it was a wildcat of some sort and that it was normal to see one about. It was very attractive and about the size of a Labrador dog. But as we were driving past quite quickly and there wasn't anything next to it to measure size against I might be a bit out about the size of it."

Michelle Brenton, Clydach

"If the photo is of the cat described in the article, it's definitely a Lynx, not a Puma. By the way a Puma is a Mountain Lion; they're different names for the same animal and there are several more."

Karl Jackson, Bolton

"About six months ago my aunty who has a farm in Carmarthenshire woke to find one of her cows dead which looked like it had been viciously attacked. Also another time one of he goats had her whole ear ripped off To this day we do not know what happened and how."

Debbie, Ammanford

22nd: Ceredigion/Wales. The farmer and his daughter saw the cat again in a field using a powerful lamping lamp. The farmer said, "It was the size of a whippet, jet black, and one of the large cat family, and the eyes shone crystal green when lights were shone at it. It just sauntered away.

25th: Hertfordshire/England. Nurse Chris Garvey, of Beaconsfield Road, Tring was riding her horse in Ashbridge Woods when she was horrified to see a terrier ripped to pieces by a "strange puma-like beast." She said, "I was out on my horse and 30 feet away. I saw a strange animal dart out of the undergrowth and attack the small dog. I heard a dog barking and there was a blood-curdling roar before the attack. There wasn't any sign of the dog's owner. The cat was like a panther or puma and twice the size of a Labrador. It had short black hair."
The attack occurred at 2.40pm, and the animal showed no fear of the horse and rider being so close by, which worried the witness even more. The witness carried on to the Livery Yard, Stocks Farm, Aldbury, and reported the incident to the police. Police said that they had no reports of any dogs fitting the description being missing. *(source: Hemel Gazette)*

29th: Buckinghamshire/England. "While on our way to Milton Keynes close to the shopping centre we saw a black panther on some wasteland adjacent to some woodland. This was a 99% genuine sighting of a large cat." After further enquiry it was found that the witnesses were about 60 ft away from the animal which was "the size of a large dog but with a feline body." *(source: Nigel Spencer – Rutland & Leicestershire Panther Watch)*

DECEMBER

3rd : Argyllshire/Scotland. Three workmen travelling North on the A83 near Tayinloan spotted a large cat which ran into the road as they were driving their van. One of them, quoted in the Campletown Courier, said, "We nearly hit it. It leapt straight over the fence and right across the road. I reckon it was about four feet long. It was too big for a domestic cat and too agile for a dog." (Member Shaun Stevens adds that the hedgerows around here are 4 – 6 feet high). *(source: Campletown Courier)*

4th: Ayrshire/Scotland. An ex-police sergeant saw a large black cat cross fields in the late afternoon. His wife also saw the cat, which at first she thought was a dog. Both, on seeing the cat move, decided that it was feline. The area is a known big cat hot spot. *(source: Brian Murphy)*

5th: Argyllshire/Scotland. During the early hours along the Tayinloan Straight a local business man travelling South saw a large black cat on the road. The animal appeared from the bushes and ran across the road and up a dirt track before disappearing into the darkness. The man's work colleague who was travelling in a car behind him also saw the animal as he turned the corner. It had actually run back across the road and disappeared into the area from which the first witness had seen it emerge. He said, "You would not believe the speed it ran at. This thing was extremely fast. It was about the size of a large Labrador dog and seemed to have a sort of hooked tail." *(source: Campletown Courier)*

circa 7th: County Sligo/Irish Republic. The Irish *Sunday Mirror* apparently carried reports of a large black cat being seen. Nor further details available.

circa 8th: Yorkshire/England. A local Oughtibridge man in North Sheffield believes this sheep was attacked by a big cat by the prints found near the carcass. The witness reported to Look Local (North Sheffield) that: "The claw marks on the side of the body were massive. The paw prints in the mud were very clear, and they were certainly those of a large animal. It was not a dog that killed the sheep. Dogs attack the head of their prey." The sheep was found just off Jaw Bone Hill, Oughtibridge, and is one of a few sheep that have been found dead under mysterious circumstances recently. *(source: Look Local)*

Insert picture (sheep remains, with leg at top)

circa 9th: County Kilkenny/Irish Republic. Reports of a large black cat spotted several times. No further details.

circa 12th: County Monaghan/Irish Republic. Tree scratches found in "unusual circumstances" near Tully. *(source: Charlie McGuinness)*

12th: Lancashire/England circa 13.00 hrs. Just South of Port Sunlight Station, The Wirral. An animal the size of a nearly full-grown Labrador, seen in rough ground alongside the railway creeping through vegetation, not moving like a dog, seen for 10 – 15 seconds, from South-bound train, from left side window (i. e. East side of railway line). *(source Martin Bailey)*

Alan Fleming followed the sighting up:

"I knew where the sighting location was and knew it to be quite a built-up area on the River (Mersey) side of the line. I wasn't familiar with the other side of the line though. It is very wooded and overgrown at the back of the massive Lever soap production complex, with houses few and far between. My wife tells me that it is more or less like that, with big houses and massive gardens and woods; oh, and of course the ubiquitous golf course, (where would big cat sightings be without the golf courses and railway lines), right up to the line of the M53 motorway where there have been several sightings on the bridges over the years. From there it is a swathe of farmland right out into Cheshire passing other known sighting locations, so it looks promising.

The other thing that I should have said is some kind of scale. It wouldn't be far off if you consider the distance from the most recent sighting to the edge of Brackenwood golf course where it meets the motorway junction as being about a kilometre (5/8ths of a mile for all the dinosaurs!)

It has always been my thought that if cats were passing through these residential areas to hunt in the woods there should be a lot more sightings. The two railways lines in the area provide the obvious answer, because they present obvious highways to the open countryside of South Wirral and Cheshire. I have attached a map showing what I mean. The shaded area is predominantly large houses with large gardens set amongst wooded areas straight back out into farmland. The map shows how the very rural areas (the beige area) come right into the middle of the Wirral Peninsula, and thus makes it very easy for these cat sightings to be in heavily built up areas, only a mile or two from Liverpool City centre (granted on the other side of the river, but you take my point).

Alan returned to the area of the sighting at least twice.

14th: Gloucestershire/England. Witness saw a large black cat lunge into rough grassland near Heywood wood, Cinderford. He at first thought it was a black Labrador. He first spotted it when he was 75 yards away and his Dalmatian ran after it. When they reached the spot where it was seen his dog "was going crazy for the smell". The witness stayed in the area for aother ten minutes but did not see the animal again.

circa 15th: Devon/England Exact location not known. Black cat, ears not large "but stompish". Approx 4ft tall while it sat back on its hind legs. "Anyone who hunts or tries to track this cat would be endangering it's life and safety. This cat, I would say, is cautious of man. It was by sheer surprise that I had the privilege to come face to face with such an extraordinary animal. How would I describe it? Well it happened amazingly by sheer surprise. At the time I happened to walk around the corner and saw what my first instinct said was a slightly larger than average black Labrador, now I am an animal lover and friend to all the animals I see, and even insects.

I have silly habits of stopping as I am walking and picking up stranded worms in silly situations. Anyway take no notice, right okay.

I saw at first in the shadowy darkness of the street lamps what looked like a big black Labrador. So I automatically walked up to it with my fingers saying "here boy" but then with the blink of an eye I realised that this thing was just as surprised as I was to the confrontation.

Shocked, I kept still thinking to myself is this thing going to bite or what, it just was silently still, unbelievable. I was a matter of three to three and a half feet away from feeding myself to a cat. I kept still and was puzzled the same as this cat was. Let me tell you something this cat is no harm at all to humans and that is a fact. If you ask me, either long ago or at some time this cats relatives possibly 10 to 15 years ago or maybe a little longer – it was I would say from its behaviour of not eating me – I would say weren't known to be harmful to him or hi past generation.

As it comes to me – he or she is an agile beautiful creature and is probably feeding off the land to which it roam's. I reckon its possible to tame such a cat as this but as you no he's very much better left alone to be happy and free as a legend. I just hope to god no pigheaded greedy thick farmer touches him or uses a gun to be a hero.

The incident ended with me stepping back a foot, the cat stood up and turned to the left and cleared a gathering pile of wood 2 to 3 foot high by five and a bit wide. Absolutely dead silent – like tip toe landed and like a ghost in the dark disappeared and the direction he went was to a small field that had no way out apart jumping and clearing the fence. No I didn't give chase... I could sketch you a picture – it looked like yellowy coloured eyes. (source: BCIB report form)

16th : Glamorgan/Wales. Three hundred chickens were slaughtered in one night at Bevexe Fawr Farm in Dunvant, it is not known what animal killed them. Most had their throats cut, some died of fear. Council officers were dispatched but confirmed that the predator had not been identified. *(source: South Wales Evening Post)*

17th: Norfolk/England Location – Near Norwich airport, TG 214156, Colour – glossy black, no markings. Long tail, curved down from the body then curved up again, slightly thicker at the end.

Three cats, about the height of Alsatians but slightly crouched. They had long sleek bodies and thick legs. I was driving North on the A140 and spotted an open field on the right standing on a raised undulation about 50 feet from the road, THREE large black cats feeding on something. They were clearly visible from the road. I'm not an expert, but they looked young, not fully grown. I turned around at the next junction to go back and photograph them, but they'd gone. I parked, but couldn't see anything more. The cats were in a field only about 1/3 rd mile North of Norwich airport on the A140, coming towards Horsham St Faith. I've had a look at black cat images to try and guess what species I think they might be, and believe they look like black jaguars of some description. However most of the pictures I found focus on the head, and the best view that I had was one of the cats side on, which made it obvious that they weren't dogs or domestic cats. *(source BCIB report form)*

17th: Gloucestershire/England Hi. Don't know if this has anything to do with big cats, but found it strange. Walking in the woods in Gloucestshire with a friend, dog and two children, we came across remains of a Roe Deer. All that was left was the top part of the skull, spine and remains of pelvic bones, one still attached, the other close by. All the ribs had been chewed off close to the spine and approximately half of the half of the dorsal spines of the vertebrae had been chewed off . The bones were fresh, still damp with blood, and the brain in the remaining portion of the skull was not dried out or shrunken, so given the local conditions, the animal could not have been killed more than 48 hours ago at the outside. The deer must have been killed elsewhere as there was no sign of blood or hair in the vicinity. Hard ground and leaf litter left no discernible clues (to my untrained eyes at least). One of the pelvic bones had a puncture that looked very much like a canine tooth hole.

An initial thought was that this could be the remains from a poaching incident that had been found by foxes or badgers. However, looking at the pelvic bones and vertebrae there were no signs of butchering marks. Also, I doubt that a poacher would have left the hid legs behind as they are the largest and most easily removed joints of meat. I have butchered a few deer myself and would never butcher out the pelvic bones like that (and even if I had disarticulated the hind leg bones there would be marks on the bones where the tendons were cut). Given the length of the spine I would guess that an animal of this size would butcher out at about 35/40 pounds, not including hide, bones and guts, so that's a lot of meat to be scavenged in a short amount of time. I have never come across anything like this before (I spend a lot of time in the woods and run courses on wild food).

Could this be a big cat kill, or should I be looking closer to home for a culprit? I would be most interested to hear if you have come across this sort of thing before.

With best regards,

Jeannie Ireland
(source: email to BCIB)

18th: Leicestershire/England. A friend of my wife saw what she thinks was a panther today in the field opposite her house. It was at 07.30 in Stathern, a village in the Vale of Belvoir, North East Leicestershire. She hunts with the Belvoir and has Labrador dogs; she initially thought it was a large lab until she saw the way it moved. She said it was like a cat, and it leapt up over the hedge in the movement of a large cat. It was black in colour and bigger than her own Labrador dogs (which are big) and about 80 yards away. Her neighbour heard a large growl like a big cat in the next field hedge the other year and there have been numerous sightings around the village and the next villages of Long Clowson and Hose *(famous as Stilton Cheese manufacturers)*

(Strathern is also where two DEFRA woodland officials reported to me their own encounter two years back (near my friends house) which some members reading this may recall prompted my amusing response (quoting their department) "you can't have seen one as they don't exist, do they..?") (source: Nigel Spencer, Leicestershire and Rutland Panther Watch)

20th: Gloucestershire/England. Between Cinderford and Coleford F.O.D., approximately 07.45 am. Black, about 2.5 feet tall, and approximately 5 feet long including tail. I was driving along the road between Cinderford and Coleford, heading towards Coleford along the A4136, when about 20 feet in front of me a black panther ran across the road. I stopped to look where it had gone but it had disappeared into the undergrowth.

20th: Warwickshire/England. Police warned residents to be on their guard after locals spotted a large cat. Steve Wain and his father spotted the animal whilst out walking his dog along the Greenway near Long Marston at about 4.00pm.
Mr. Wain said, "We both have a good knowledge of local and British wildlife. This animal was nothing we recognised and was clearly a big cat. We watched for five to ten minutes as the animal walked slowly towards the airfield, stopping periodically to look back."

The animal eventually leapt into a crop of maize and that was the last they saw of it. The animal was described as 2ft high, red/brown with a white chest, and having a 3ft long body and a slender, curved 2.5 ft tail. *(source: Midweek Her-*

ald)

23rd: Bedfordshire/England 3.55pm, Eaton Gray. A completely black cat with a long tail hanging down. The tail was large, the ears couldn't be seen. The witness was walking through a field with his girlfriend, and he noticed in the opposite field a large cat like creature running away from his location into some bushes. He saw it only for a split second and is unsure of the details. Quite sure that it was not a dog because of its cat-like run. It was quite far away, there was no one else around for some distance. *(source: Iain Grant by email – BCIB report form)*

www.bigcatsinbritain.org

This is a brief run down of the most active members. We have many members who take a passive interest. The group does need more contacts throughout the country. You do not need any experience as help will be gladly given.

- Honoury life president - Nigel Brierly.
- Zoological consultant - Chris Moiser.
- Photographic consultant - Paul Crowther.
- Membership secretary - Andy Williams.
- Vigil & expedition organiser - Mark Fraser

Media contacts.

- South England - Alan White.
- North England - Mark Fraser
- South and Central Scotland - Brian Murphy.
- Argyllshire - Shaun Stephens.
- N Ireland & Eire - Mark Fraser

We have members and friends in the following counties:

Flintshire, Yorkshire, Renfrewshire, Ayrshire, Merseyside, London and surrounding counties, Irish Republic, Kent, Essex, Hampshire, Lanca-shire, Leicestershire, West Sussex, Sutherland, Falkirk, Wales, Warwick-shire, Northumberland, Dorset, Gloucestershire, Dumfries-shire, Lincoln-shire, Humberside, Argyllshire, Cambridgeshire.

Overseas researchers are based in Australia, USA, Italy and the Netherlands.

Websites

www.scottishbigcats.org
www.bigcatsinbritain
http://myhome.iolfree.ie/~dorsetbigcats/index.htm
http://www.cfz.org.uk/cats
http://www.bigcats.org.uk
http://www.pcfe.ac.uk/cats/index.html
http://www.lochnessinvestigation.org/Pumas.html
http://www.matmice.com/home/black_cats_uk
http://www.big-cats.co.uk
http://www.webace.com.au/~pwest/marca
http://www.beastwatch.co.uk
http://www.wildlifeservices.org.uk
http://www.strokestownpoetryprize.com
http://www.writer.utvinternet.com

Membership to BCIB is £12 annually:

- A BCIB membership certificate.
- Access to the members area.
- A personal webpage.
- Two colour newsletters, glossy covered.
- Access to the members only mailing list where you will be constantly updated on what is happening when and where.
- Discounts on any products the group sells.
- Updated information of sightings in your area, along with the chance of investigating locally on our behalf, and more importantly with our back-up.
- Please include a passport sized picture for your ID card.
- Listed on the website as an investigator for your area (Please do not waste your and our time unless you really are prepared to become a contact, it does require some effort, but it is worth it).
- A chance to attend the vigils we hold every year in the hope of finding some real evidence.
- The opportunity to attend social events .
- An A4 print of your favourite cat.
- Templates for sightings forms, prints, faeces finds, logs etc.
- How to sheets ... and much more all presented in a 40 page A4 booklet.

Please make cheques made payable to *Mark Fraser*

Big Cats in Britain
35 South Dean Road
Kilmarnock, Ayrshire
KA3 7RD

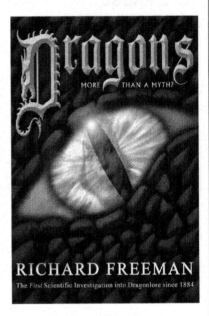

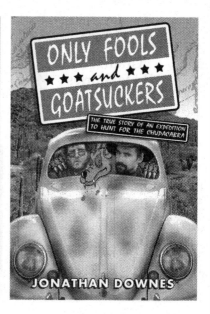

Other books available from
CFZ PRESS

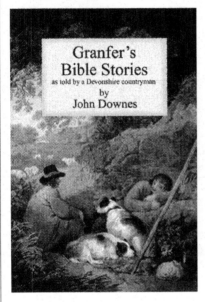

GRANFER'S BIBLE STORIES

Bible stories in the Devonshire vernacular, each story being told by an old Devon Grandfather - 'Granfer'. These stories are now collected together in a remarkable book presenting selected parts of the Bible as one more-or-less continuous tale in short 'bite sized' stories intended for dipping into or even for bed-time reading. `Granfer` treats the biblical characters as if they were simple country folk living in the next village. Many of the stories are treated with a degree of bucolic humour and kindly irreverence, which not only gives the reader an opportunity to re-evaluate familiar tales in a new light, but do so in both an entertaining and a spiritually uplifting manner.

ISBN 0-9512872-8-1

FRAGRANT HARBOURS DISTANT RIVERS

Many excellent books have been written about Africa during the second half of the 19th Century, but this one is unique in that it presents the stories of a dozen different people, whose interlinked lives and achievements have as many nuances as any contemporary soap opera. It explains how the events in China and Hong Kong which surrounded the Opium Wars, intimately effected the events in Africa which take up the majority of this book. The author served in the Colonial Service in Nigeria and Hong Kong, during which he found himself following in the footsteps of one of the main characters in this book; Frederick Lugard – the architect of modern Nigeria.

ISBN 0-9512872-5-7

Lightning Source UK Ltd.
Milton Keynes UK
UKOW01f0842110717
305101UK00005B/224/P